This is an honest and beautiful portrait of two people opening to themselves and each other; each releasing themselves from ways of being that have kept them imprisoned. It's a beautiful book and so well written.

—Robin Swicord, writer of
"The Curious Case of Benjamin Button"

This book is an unexpected little gem. It puts the depth of Anamika's work into a light and joyous context that's totally enjoyable to read.

—Carrie Zivetz, Actress

It is exquisite!! This is a guidebook for relationships (certainly it will be for mine) and a completely fresh way of relating in a new paradigm. In celebration of a triumphant piece of brilliance!

—Sue Kiel, Theater Maker

I love it! So funny, full of delight, sexy, deep, warm and vulnerable. It's an entertaining and easy read that left me wanting to know what happens next.

—Sandi Stuart, Agency Licensing

Also by Anamika

Loving Now

Love in Fur Coats: Gifts from my animal companions

and...

French Lessons in Love

...and some lessons in language too

Anamika

Cover design and photo by Norman Seeff
Author photo by Norman Seeff
Edited by Carrie Zivetz
Formatted by Karen Richardson

More information at www.anamika.com

ISBN: 978-0-9908379-1-6

French Lessons in Love...and some lessons in language too / Anamika.

CONTENTS

thanks

To my dear Zacharie for being such a beautiful man, and for deeply impacting my life in so many extraordinary ways.

To Carrie Zivetz for your creative contribution and superb editing.

To Norman Seeff for your exquisite photography, book cover design, and friendship.

To Karen Richardson for your excellent formatting and epublishing.

To Irene Mink, for your vision of this material as a book and compassionate friendship.

To Lilou Mace for encouraging me to write.

To Robin Swicord and Tom Schulman for generous guidance in the writing process.

To Barbara Hamilton, Katerina Getchell, Jennifer and Michael Goodrich, Lisheyna Hurvitz, Steve Parrish, Barnet Bain, Stephan Choiniere, Rick Sugarman, Andrew and LeAnna Wollenberg, Liora Mendeloff, Leerone Milstein, Sue Kiel, Barbara Tfank and Sandi Stuart for the deep friendship, wise guidance and personal support that helped me realize this book.

To Penelope Smith and Nancy Rosenquist for your special friendship with Shaqqara.

To Yitka Hamilton for raising Thor and generously sharing him.

To Shaqqara and Thor for being themselves.

To Eleanor, Mark, Jill, Susan and Peter Neitlich, Barbara Broder, and Ellen Stein for being such a loving family.

To Daryl Baucum for generously transcribing.

"I want to fill you with my energy, giving you more and more pleasure everywhere until you're overflowing with light and joy." Zacharie

« Je veux te combler avec mon énergie, de donner de plus en plus de plaisir par tous les pores de ta peau, jusqu'à ce que tu sois submergée par la lumière et la joie. » Zacharie

Anamika:
Hi cutie pie, I'm at the computer writing our story and I'm almost at the end.

Zacharie:
I hope the end of the book is not the end of the story. It's a living story that never ends.

Anamika:
I'm calling it *French Lessons in Love ...and some lessons in language too.*

Zacharie:
But I don't really need French lessons!

Anamika:
No, you don't! I'm the one who needs French lessons, and especially the ones you give me that I don't even know I need!*

* A black box around a conversation indicates a text message throughout the book.

CHAPTER 1

voulez-vous coucher avec moi ?

For some mysterious reason, I felt an inexplicable desire to learn French. The sensuality and romance of the language had captivated me since I studied it in high school. I wanted to experience its fluidity, music, and rhythm again.

I could barely speak French, except to name the days of the week, and of course, "*Voulez-vous coucher avec moi?*" Do you want to sleep with me?

I live in Malibu, a gorgeous town overlooking the sea, with my dog Shaqqara. She has been my cherished companion for the past thirteen years. I love what I do, working with people one on one and in workshops, supporting their spiritual and psychological growth.

The sort of work I do by its very nature requires that I am always growing, exploring and evolving.

It's exciting work, full of the mystery and adventure of pioneering human consciousness. Sounds great, right? It is! However, I had been feeling restless and found myself daydreaming about my life going in a new direction. One afternoon, I wondered why not study French?

I tend to be rather private about my personal life, and here I am, signing up with an online language community to learn French. Totally outside my comfort zone!

Every night I would go to my computer, log on, and sit there worried about my mediocre French. Shaqqara wondered why I was at the computer until so late every night. After two weeks of studiously learning the written lessons, I worked up the courage to chat with a sexy young Moroccan man. He had persistently requested a chat every night for a week.

I was awkward about my French, but his English was far worse. "Show me your body," he kept saying, indicating he wanted me to stand up in front of my monitor. As tempting as this hot young stud was, I realized I would learn nothing but French words for sex. So, I abandoned the chat room idea and continued with the written lessons.

A month into my mysterious passion for French, I was contacted by a French Physics professor. His profile included a photo of himself seated, with a basket over his head! I wondered if French was right for me after all!!

*

Hi, I'm Zacharie. I'm a Physics professor and I have to improve my English. Can you help me?

I wondered what was underneath the basket. Then he sent me his written lessons in English to correct, and I realized he was sincere. So I sent him back an audio recording in English, correcting his mistakes.

Anamika,
Your audio recording was very useful. I'd be happy

* An envelope indicates an email.

to help you in French. Would you like to try it on Skype?

Zacharie

I was intrigued, but why was he under a basket? What was he hiding? Even though I had signed up for a language course, if I'm going to be honest with myself, I was hoping that underneath the basket would be a tall, sexy Frenchman.

I needed to know more before exposing myself to Skype, so I emailed him back, trying out my rudimentary French.

✉

Zacharie,
I live in Malibu. Where do you live?

Anamika

✉

Anamika,
I live in a small town located about 30 km north of Paris. My eyesight is not good enough to see the Eiffel Tower through the window of my house. So

I have to enhance both my pronunciation and my eyesight! I am sure you will be able to help me for English language, not sure you can do something for my eyes!

You write in French excellent! I am afraid to make much more mistakes than you did. I wish you will show me what is wrong in my writing.

Zacharie

The basket on his head had me convinced he must be shy, insecure about his looks, or a clown. But, there was something in his quirky humor that made me want to know more.

Hello Zacharie,
I can definitely help with your English. I may not be able to help improve your eyesight, but I may be able to help improve your vision. It must be hard to see clearly, on so many levels, with a basket over your head! What's under the basket?

Anamika

✉

Anamika,
Let's meet on Skype and you can see.
Zacharie

The first time we met on Skype, he showed up without the basket, looking quite shy. He was balding, with unkempt salt and pepper hair, and blue eyes. He had the demeanor of a self-effacing but very intelligent, absent-minded professor. He was not the Adonis I was hoping for, but there was something appealing about him that intrigued me.

I asked him why he decided to contact me. Was it my picture? When he said no, I was offended, certain he found me unattractive. Secretly, I had hoped my picture was sexy enough to attract a handsome Frenchman.

I asked him why he didn't like the picture. He said it looked posed and unnatural, not free and relaxed the way I looked in person on Skype.

Okay...good answer...and I was impressed by his perceptiveness. The picture had been taken by a

Vogue photographer, at the home of a well-known Hollywood actress/model, who was a dear friend. I remember observing the ease with which my friend, the model, posed for the camera, as I myself grew increasingly insecure. I felt anything but sexy. I wished I could appear on camera as natural and beautiful as she.

Once in front of the camera, I froze. It was as if I had just been plunked down in the middle of a performance by the New York City ballet, wearing street clothes, clunky shoes, and supposed to pirouette twenty times. I was painfully aware of trying to look "right" for the pictures, instead of just being myself.

I admitted to Zacharie that I froze when I had my picture taken. But I wanted to know why he had contacted me again, if not because of the picture. He said that something lovely and warm in my voice captured his interest in my audio recording. During this first conversation, Zacharie told me he was in a relationship with a woman he had been living with for almost 25 years. What a relief! Since he wasn't my prince charming, we could get down to French lessons.

Zacharie told me he had had sexual proposals from women on the language site. I told him about the Moroccan and we laughed. He said he was relieved to find someone intelligent and committed to learning, with whom he could get down to English lessons.

Mysteriously, he had felt an urgency to learn English at the same time I felt a passion to learn French. Serendipitously, he signed up for the online language site exactly when I had. We were perfectly matched in our rudimentary language skills. His charming awkwardness in English made my fumbling French more tolerable.

Zacharie was very confused about his sudden interest in English because his childhood experiences with it had been traumatic. He hesitantly sent me his first blog:

This is the first page of my first blog. Never, I have thought that one day I would write a blog in English and, above all, I would enjoy writing it! Sometimes, life follows strange ways.

When I was 10 years old, I had my first contact with English. I was very excited because I was curious to learn new things.

As soon as the teacher knew my last name, he demanded me to sit at the back of the class. I am the last child in my family and this teacher had had my four brothers before me, and then was prejudiced against me!

In the classroom, he was never smiling, never telling something sweet to the pupils. He was constantly looking like angry. I was feeling almost sick every time I was in the classroom with him.

For four never-ending years he was my English teacher. First I began to hate him, then I began to hate English, at last I began to hate school in general.

A few years after my higher education, I noticed that I really needed to improve my English. I was keen on science, and all the most interesting science magazines were written in English. So, I had to read English books, hence I did it.

For more than 20 years, I have been torn between two conflicting feelings. I was attracted by English language, the key to unlocking a fascinating and extensive world. But, while I was reading English, I could see superimposed, the stern face of my teacher. While I was listening to English, I could hear his sarcastic reproaches.

Maybe it's unusual to begin a blog with such a sad narrative, but I feel in my bones that I won't be able to go forward until this page has been turned.

I am not naïve, I don't believe in miracles, but I have probably met the right person at the right moment to help with an important change in my life.

Let's finish the story in a more lightweight tone. There are two fall-outs, not so bad in fact, of my teacher's behavior. First, he taught me something very important: how I should NOT behave towards my pupils to be reasonably good at my job, and it improved my relationship with my dog.

Because of my teacher, I was so ashamed to speak English in the classroom that I have hardly ever spoken. You can guess how bad is my pronunciation and how strong is my accent. The only one who understands me when I speak English is my dog. That's why we are now such good friends, and as a result I became an expert at pronunciation of the consonant "R," the doggy sound "grrrrrrr," like in the word "were." I am very proud, because pronouncing "r" in English is attempting the impossible for French people!

Lastly, I should be grateful to my teacher, but strangely I am not!

Zacharie,
You have expressed many complex thoughts in English. Good for you! I'm touched that you have let me know about your early experiences. Below are my corrections, the most important ones in CAPITAL LETTERS:

Because of my teacher, I was so ashamed to speak English in the classroom that I have hardly ever spoken. You can guess how bad my pronunciation is (NO, IT'S NOT!) and how strong my accent is (IT'S CHARMING AND NOT SO STRONG!!). The only one who understands me when I speak English is my dog (YOU DON'T HAVE A DOG, YOU TOLD ME YOU HAD TWO CATS!!). That's why we are now such good friends and as a result I became an expert at the pronunciation of the consonant "R,"the doggy sound "grrrrrrr" like in the word "were." I am very proud, because pronouncing "r" in English is attempting the impossible for French people! (YOU SHOULD HEAR MY R's IN FRENCH!! I SOUND LIKE I'M CHOKING ON A WALNUT!!!)

Anamika

I could see how proud he was of his first blog in English. I was proud of him too. It was like watching a child who is learning to walk fall down and dare to get up again. In return for correcting his blog, he made me an audio recording of a few paragraphs of his favorite book, *Le Petit Prince.* I read this book in high school French class and it is my favorite, too.

As he read a passage in French, his voice on the recording was filled with such authentic emotion, it sounded like music to me; such a resonant voice, in my favorite language, reading from my favorite childhood book. I cried my heart out from the sheer beauty and magic of it all. How could such emotion be coming from this shy Physics professor who reminded me so much of my neighbor's dog, Thor?

I should explain. A handsome, Scandinavian God, Thor is not. He is a medium sized black fuzzy thing, with endearing golden eyes. Zacharie was also medium sized with fuzzy hair, warm eyes and an endearing smile.

In spite of Thor's lack of pedigree, he is my dog Shaqqara's best friend. If I were ever jealous of anyone's looks, it would be Shaqqara. A stunning and regal Afghan Hound, with flowing golden hair, Shaqqara turns heads. Dubbed "The super model of Malibu beach," I can go nowhere without people gasping at her exquisite beauty and elegant bearing.

Shortly after her equally statuesque brother, Shalim, died quite suddenly, Thor showed up on our doorstep. I had no idea where he came from. When Thor first laid eyes on Shaqqara, it was love at first sight. His eyes became soft and round, and his heart melted. She, on the other hand, looked down her long aristocratic nose at this dusty burr covered mop, and turned away, barely acknowledging his presence. Despite Shaqqara's aloofness, with dogged determination Thor showed up day after day. Finally, I called the phone number on his dog tag.

His "mom" said she had noticed a big change in him, as if he had fallen in love. She was happy for him to come visit. Running through the brush to see Shaqqara, he arrived daily covered with dust and weeds. Since he was quite obviously smitten and determined to see his new love, I threw him in the tub for a good scrubbing. Five shampoos later, his black fur was glistening. He strutted proudly in front of Shaqqara, feeling ever so handsome. She approved of his new look by noticing him.

While Thor didn't have the elegant bearing of Shalim, his heart was wide open. He greeted everyone with a big toothy grin and they fell in love with him right away. Many people reported him audibly saying, "I love you." Finally, even Shaqqara admitted that Thor made her laugh. He became her best friend and constant companion.

In a similar fashion, Zacharie and I spent a good deal of our time laughing together. His quirky humor was charming and made me laugh. Once I told him he was funny and he said it was because he ate a little clown for breakfast every morning.

He turned out to be an exceptional teacher, and not only in the French language. My French lessons went far beyond what I had expected. Likewise, his lessons in English surprised and liberated him, changing his life forever.

CHAPTER 2

the first kiss?

We conversed daily in French and English. Since there was no formal structure, we followed our creative whims. Being a Physics professor, Zacharie was oriented toward learning through formal exercises. Being in the fields of Psychology and Awakening Consciousness, I was oriented toward relating and exploring.

Hello Anamika,

Pour ta leçon de français: For your French lesson, I will give you many ways to say that the moments we have spent together in discussion have been agreeable:

> ➢*Plaisant:* You can say that the time we have spent together has been very pleasant.

➢*Apprécier:* Another way of saying it would be that I have appreciated spending time in your company. That's prettier.

➢*Avoir du plaisir:* Or, I had a lot of pleasure conversing with you.

➢*Savourer:* Finally, you can say that I have savored the moments we have spent together.

I hope this lesson pleases you and that you have learned some vocabulary.

Zacharie

✉

Zacharie,

You are certainly quite the Physics professor! You are as exact and precise with your language as you must be with your science, so I am learning quite a bit of French vocabulary.

However, I am very direct. So, can we talk about how we feel directly, not just theoretically? I would like to know how you feel about the time we spend together. I am eager to learn the vocabulary of your heart, not only that of your head.

✉

Hello Anamika,

I was very interested in what you said in your email *à propos du cœur*, about the heart. Because you are oriented toward feelings, I have chosen some words for you in French:

➢*Affection:* To have affection for someone means to like that person in the sense of friendship.

➢*Amour:* If you want to speak of love, it is not a superficial affection for someone, but a deep affection.

➢*Chérir:* The last word to learn today is when the affection is like a live being that needs care. We cherish it, nourish it and do the necessary things so that the affection continues to live.

Just as Zacharie had a gift for teaching, for clarifying the most abstruse aspects of Physics, I have a gift of intuition and connecting with another person. Since I was a child, I've been able to feel the presence of a person's essence communicate with me telepathically and through the movement of energy within and around my body. I could always feel another person's emotions, intentions and desires. I sense them so intimately that it's like touching their soul. I utilize these gifts in the work I do, helping people grow.

Zacharie,

As usual, this was a fascinating exercise in French, but it's still indirect. I want to know personally how you feel. You might not be used to such directness but please tell me your feelings straight from the heart. That's how I can get to know you.

My expectation had been to learn French. But with Zacharie I felt compelled to explore something deeper than language. I knew I was focusing on drawing out his feelings without yet sharing my own. But I sensed if I were too forthcoming, too soon, he might run screaming into the night, and I didn't want to cause that! *Je prenais des gants.* So… with kid gloves.

Hello Anamika,

I was very interested in what you said in your email about being direct. So I prepared a little exercise for you regarding a conversation between two people. In French, when we use the casual term *"tu"* instead of the formal *"vous"* for "you" with a person, it means the two people are close.

Zacharie,

You have been using the casual term *"tu"* from the beginning. Does this mean you feel we are close enough to share our feelings? I know you're a professor, but I wonder if your choice of the vocabulary you're teaching me is what you're really feeling? Or perhaps not, maybe they're just exercises? ;-)

Anamika

I sensed sharing his feelings might not be something he was accustomed to. After all, he was a professor of Physics, not of love. However, each time I made playful suggestions, he cautiously responded. We spoke on Skype.

Zacharie:
Between us we have two languages, so we have more than one option for expressing feelings.

Anamika:
We have three languages, French, English and resonance. Actually, we have four, *inventisme.*

Zacharie:
This is not a word in French.

Anamika:
I made it up! It means when I don't know the word, I invent one. It's how I overcome my frustration of not being able to say what I truly want to in French.

Zacharie:
I don't speak *"inventisme,"* and I don't speak resonance. Therefore, in both of these languages I don't understand you.

Anamika:
Maybe you don't speak "inventisme" but you do speak resonance. You're a Physics professor! Can't you feel the resonance of my communication even when you don't understand the words?

Zacharie:
I think you're using words like resonance in a different way than I do in my work, but, yes, I do seem to understand you intuitively. However, it's easier to understand someone when you can see their face and hear their voice. It's not the same thing to say, *"Je t'aime,"* "I love you," casually as to say, *"Oh, je t'aime,"* deeply, with an entirely different tone of voice.

Anamika:
Is this another exercise you're giving me or are you actually telling me how you feel?

Zacharie:
I can't define how I feel. There is no explanation. You are you and I am me.

Anamika:
Well, whatever it is, it certainly isn't the "L" word, haha!

Zacharie:
Ah! Ah!

After this Skype exchange, Zacharie went away on vacation in the Alps with Sabine for a month. Before leaving, he told me he was afraid I would find another French speaking person to connect with and would forget him. I assured him that this would not be the case. He wasn't reassured.

Even though I wanted him to be direct with his feelings, I didn't tell him I would miss him. So I suggested if he wanted to continue to practice his English, he could contact me. He said it might be difficult because he would be in the mountains, with very limited cell phone and Internet access.

The very next day, however, a text in his adorable English arrived:

Z: Hi! I am arrived. The weather is awful but my personal weather is good. I already miss our talks.
A: *Bonjour, mon ami.* Hello my friend. I miss you too.

The next day, another text arrived:

> **Z:** Bad news, the neighbor's dog here in the mountains died. I will miss two things during my holidays: talking with the dog and walking with you.
> **A:** I am sorry that you can no longer talk to the dog or walk with me. *Je suis triste sans toi.* I am sad without you. I miss you in French and in English.

I missed connecting with him but tried to convince myself that I didn't. What a lifelong repetitive story this has been: dreaming of "The One," never finding "The One," and then pretending it doesn't matter.

"The One" is the way I've come to define the perfect man, Prince Charming, that elusive romantic fantasy of a soul mate who would meet all of my needs and sweep me off of my feet. Guess what? He hasn't shown up yet. But that didn't prevent me from hoping that one day he would.

On the third day of Zacharie's vacation, I was lying on my living room couch. It was an overcast day in Malibu. I was missing Zacharie and feeling blue. Suddenly, I felt his presence as clearly as if he were physically in the room.

Zacharie's gentle masculine presence approached me softly. He looked in my eyes and gave me the most tender, deep kiss I have ever experienced. His energy infused me, filling my whole being. I was astounded by his passion. It was so strong it overwhelmed me with joy. At that moment, the sun broke through the clouds filling the room with light.

The next day, I got a text from him asking me to call him at a phone booth in the mountains. He bicycled in the heat to wait for my call.

Our first conversation by phone, strangely enough, made our relationship seem more real. Previously we had only spoken by Skype or exchanged emails and texts. Speaking by phone added another dimension to our communication. Without the visual, we had to focus on each other's voice and resonance. As a result, we felt each other more intensely.

During this conversation, I could feel once again his tender presence.

```
A: I felt a new, special connection between us since our phone call.
Z: I did too, and I miss your news and our talks.
```

I put down my iPhone and realized I was in a quandary. I could still feel the deliciousness of his kiss on my lips. How was that possible if he was not "The One?"

I was ready for a relationship with a man, but he was already in a relationship. Also, despite the growing feelings of connection between us, I wasn't attracted to him in that way. However, we seemed to have something between us I can only describe as deep soul chemistry. I was very confused.

At the same time, Zacharie was beginning to realize how important I was to him. He rode his bicycle up and down the Alps in 100-degree heat in order to be alone to speak with me. He clearly wanted to keep our relationship going.

I wanted to tell him about the kiss experience, but was reluctant because I didn't think he would believe me, and might think I was crazy. I wasn't ready to admit how much I wanted to connect with him like that, despite the lack of physical attraction. I didn't understand this push/pull inside of me. Also, revealing my gifts of perceiving energy, and my unconventional way of life has alienated men in the past.

Even though I've had these "kiss" experiences before, never with this intensity or depth. I was conflicted, but couldn't hold back the power of the experience. So, I told him I'd had a dream in which he had passionately kissed me.

He was very surprised. He thought I understood he wasn't available, and he had never considered I might be interested in him in that way. He was right, I wasn't. But despite my disinterest, I was having very intense feelings every time I connected with him.

When I told him about the dream, he confessed he was blushing. But being a good scientist, he immediately tried to find a logical reason for the dream.

Then, I risked telling him that maybe it was a real energy experience and not just a dream.

He thought that if it was an energy experience, it was a little crazy. I was used to that response, but what was different is that Zacharie didn't back away. The moment he got home, he called me on Skype.

He confessed that he had been thinking about my "dream" and that the kiss was probably what he longed for too. However, he was already in a 25-year relationship. Now, he was confused. He had thought of our relationship as a language exchange, and suddenly something unexpected was happening.

He had not told Sabine that he was studying English with a woman. He explained that she can be rather insecure and wouldn't believe the relationship was only about language. Also, he and Sabine didn't want to know about other people. Before my dream, it would have made no difference to him studying English with a man or woman. But now…

Something was beginning to change. Our conversations and our relationship were moving into territory neither of us anticipated or even wanted. I couldn't see our relationship becoming a "real" relationship but I was drawn to getting closer. At the same time, it began to dawn on him that his relationship with Sabine had stagnated. The chemistry and the magic had disappeared years ago.

This didn't surprise me. When he spoke of Sabine, I couldn't sense any emotional or sexual connection between them. He felt single to me. He eventually admitted they had not been sexual for over a year and slept in separate rooms. In our conversations, he began to recognize that there was something more he was seeking, and that's why he had drawn me into his life.

Zacharie:
I feel like part of me is with you and part of me is living here with Sabine. Five years ago we agreed to have an open relationship, but I never expected that I would meet someone. Now it's like I have two separate lives that are completely different.

Anamika:
Oh, you have an open relationship? That makes me feel so much better about connect-

ing with you. I can sense you are torn between two different worlds. That must be so hard.

A crucial turning point came when Zacharie admitted that while he wasn't ready to let go of his relationship with Sabine, internally he already had. Like me, he was utterly perplexed.

CHAPTER 3

what a strange relationship

I didn't know how to resolve my contradictory feelings, so I went about the business of trying to help him express his. This was another old coping strategy. But, given his confusion, he wasn't ready to deal with mine as well.

Bonjour Anamika,

I had a long day of classes, which were tiring because it's very hot in France right now and hard to concentrate on Physics.

Zacharie,

In the interest of learning direct communication,

here's what I heard you actually say in your email: I had a long day of classes, which were tiring because my emotions are heating up inside of me. It's hard to concentrate on Physics because I'm thinking about you.

How's my hearing?

Anamika

✉

Hello Anamika,

Your ears are working perfectly. You are exactly right about my feelings, I dare say. How can you read me so clearly? Am I that transparent?

Zacharie

✉

Zacharie,

Luckily for both of us, yes you are!

Anamika

Chère Anamika,

Now I am even more curious about you, because you seem to know what I am feeling before I do. So I have just watched two of your videos on your website which describe your work. They were surprising and interesting. Surprising, because sometimes it seemed to me we were speaking the same language. I don't mean French, but something beyond. Interesting, because I am starting to understand your world. I like the way you explain the infinite connection we all have, and the metaphor that we are the ocean of love and limitless possibility itself.

Zacharie,

Have you noticed that when you are connecting to your feelings, your English improves?

Anamika,

Yes, and I've also noticed when I am speaking English, my feelings improve! I'm beginning to see that the key to life is not just in the head, it might be in the feelings too.

Zacharie

Each time he took another step forward, so did I. I decided it was okay to share a little of how I felt about him.

Zacharie,

I have a love for you that is true and real, without expectation and without need. It's "just because!" It comes from a space of infinite freedom and limitless possibility. I love you without needing our relationship to take any particular form. I love you without conditions and without definition. Our relationship is not a thing to me. It's a living process, a co-creation that grows and evolves.

✉

Ma chère Anamika,

I am very touched by your feelings, even though I am shocked. I am not sure that the love you're talking about is a love I have ever experienced. You always seem to feel these things before I do. If I'm honest with myself, I feel the same way, but it's somewhere deep inside me.

Zacharie

After this revealing exchange, we rushed to the computer every day to reconnect with each other. It was like we had been hungry for a long time and our connection was food for the soul.

Zacharie:
I am so grateful for all the good things you have brought into my life. I hope we will have a long journey together through the mountains and meadows of our deep feelings.

I listened to the recording you sent me today and I laughed. It began in English for me to learn vocabulary, but by the end it was entirely in French. I see French is starting to come more naturally for you.

Anamika:
As English is for you. For me, French is the language of love, so when French comes out of my mouth, it's me loving you.

Zacharie:
C'est la plus étrange des relations que j'ai jamais eu! This is the strangest relationship I've ever had! We have never met in person, only via Skype. But, our relationship seems more real than any I've had, and yet not real at all. I say this only from my mind, because in my heart it's so real. There is a big contrast between the happiness I feel in my heart and the disconnection I feel in my mind.

Even though we have a time difference of nine hours, and you're not here physically, I am closer to you than I have ever felt to anyone. It's very confusing for me.

It's easier to spend time with Sabine and other people because they're here in the same time zone. But when I'm with them, I notice that my heart is not as open. When I spend time with you, it opens my heart.

This is very strange, because I thought that being physically with someone is the strongest kind of connection. Yet, we have an emotional connection that's stronger than anything I've experienced physically. I dream that one day you and I can have both.

Anamika:
Since we're not together physically, we need to rely on connecting emotionally and verbally. Would you be interested in connecting in another way too?

Zacharie:
How? You mean that energy thing you do in your work? I don't want to be your client or student...

Anamika:
I don't want you to either, but it could bring us closer, because you can feel energy as strongly as if we were together physically.

Zacharie:
I don't think anything could be as strong as the physical.

Anamika:
We could connect using energy. Are you open to experiencing that?

Zacharie:
This sounds very weird, but I'll try it because I trust you.

Anamika:
Ok, sit back in your chair and stay open to sensing your own energy.

Zacharie:
Mais je ne sais pas comment ressentir cette énergie. But, I don't know how to sense my energy.

Anamika:
Can you allow yourself to receive the energy I'm transmitting?

Apparently, he could, because within a minute or two I could see he was visibly vibrating as torrents of energy coursed through his body.

Zacharie was so moved, he couldn't speak for over half an hour. When he finally did, a mystic poet spoke:

Zacharie:
I feel like I'm floating in an eternal womb, in a

warm sea of amniotic fluid. Gentle waves of light are pulsing through me as I'm merging into an infinite sea of love. I feel in love in a way as never before. But this is not ordinary love. It has the flavor of eternity.

Anamika:
You're experiencing your own expanded consciousness. You're in a state of infinite love.

Even though people are generally deeply impacted by this transmission of energy, I was astonished that he opened up so quickly. I was thrilled to discover his capacity for experiencing his own infinite nature. In these realms of higher consciousness, there is a deep feeling of love and connection, but not in the conventional way of falling in love.

I was excited to have shared this with him, because now we could begin to relate in a way that was even more meaningful. In these realms beyond ordinary love, we could have truly satisfying exchanges. I hoped he felt as I did.

There isn't a word that expresses this infinite love. It would be like attempting to express the inexpressible. It is impossible to describe experiences of the infinite, and what it feels like to connect in a field of shared consciousness.

In English, like in French, we have words for different kinds of love, like affection, affinity, fondness, caring, and tenderness. But there is not a singular word for experiences of infinite love when we connect in that vast, eternal place.

CHAPTER 4

rivers of honey

Zacharie:
I just got home from Paris and couldn't wait to talk to you about what happened yesterday. When I felt the energy so deeply and intensely, it was very surprising and amazing. I've never felt so good in my life! I couldn't believe it. I just couldn't believe it! But today somehow I'm strangely disturbed and upset.

Anamika:
It's normal to have a contraction after a very intense expansion. I'm wondering what seems so disturbing about living in that kind of love?

Zacharie:
I think I will have to make a choice between two different worlds and I don't feel ready to make that choice.

Anamika:
You don't need to make a choice between me and Sabine. I'm not looking for that kind of

relationship with you. I don't know where this will lead, but I want to keep exploring these delicious feelings with you, and rest assured, I'm not looking to be your girlfriend.

Zacharie:
That's a relief because I'm not ready to make any concrete changes in my life.

Anamika:
Changes in your life don't need to be external. They can be internal. You are making internal changes when your energy is flowing and your heart is open. Change is a gradual process, a bit like arctic ice melting, a little at a time.

Zacharie:
Okay, I understand I don't need to choose between the two of you, but I'm afraid that my choice to spend more time with you will take away from my time with Sabine.

But on the other hand, compared to what you and I share, my time with her feels empty and is from guilt and obligation.

Anamika:
It seems to me that the real choice you're fac-

ing right now is between your own aliveness and your own deadness.

Zacharie:
Oui, tu as raison. Yes, you're right. I've been counting how many times you're right and we are up to number 238.

Anamika:
You've been counting?

Zacharie:
I'm a science professor. I'm used to being precise and in my head. Being in my heart is what I most want, but what I most fear because there's no precision. It's all unknown.

Anamika:
I get scared each time I stretch further into the unknown too. But, you're completely safe in the unknown. And fear and resistance are normal. Do you remember you told me about your student who was sick and missed a whole trimester? You tutored him for free. You have an extraordinarily compassionate heart. Can you give this compassion to yourself?

Zacharie:
It's easy to do for others but not for myself.

Right now I am more aware than ever that a part of me really deeply wants to open up. Yet, another part of me strongly doesn't want to. So, there's a fight between the two parts of me.

For the next several days there was a struggle between his head and his heart, to choose me, or Sabine. I didn't want him to feel pressured to choose one relationship over another. I just wanted to keep exploring with him.

He was so receptive to our journey together and the most authentic and emotionally present man I had ever known. I didn't want to lose him.

Zacharie:
I know the work you do with your clients and what we're doing together helps change your inner life, but I actually feel the need to change my outer life too.

Anamika:
I'm happy to hear that! What changes do you want?

Zacharie:
That's hard for me to share with you because sometimes I censor myself. I am a bit shy and afraid if I express my feelings, it will lead to something…

Anamika:
Something wonderful?

Zacharie:
Something I really want but think is impossible. If I express my feelings and I can't have what I really want in our relationship, I might end up very frustrated. So I don't express all of my feelings.

Anamika:
You seem frustrated right now. You could feel lighter and freer if you told me how you really feel.

Zacharie:
It's not that easy for me. With you I am less shy than with anyone else because I feel so accepted. You are the one with whom I share more about my life than anyone. But even so, I'm not used to speaking about a certain area of my life… my sexuality. And I want to be able to tell you everything.

Uh oh… I didn't see that one coming. But with the level of intimacy that was being shared between us, I wasn't paying attention to the obvious signals. I was as confused as he. To be honest, we were both having deep emotional and sexual feelings.

I had to ask myself what I really wanted here. Here was my dilemma. I was falling in love with our energy exchange and he seemed to be falling in love with me. On the one hand I wanted even more exchange of energy between us, including sexual energy. But because of Sabine and the distance between us, I naively assumed that we would never meet and could enjoy this new kind of communion without the entanglements of a daily relationship. But the strength of our connection was much too compelling.

Zacharie:
I don't want to hide anything, but I just don't dare be explicit about sexuality. I prefer to say it using poetry or to physically do what I feel.

Anamika:
Those are beautiful ways of expressing, but perhaps we can open up another dimension of possibility here.

Zacharie:
I don't know what you mean.

Anamika:
I would definitely like a deeper exchange of energy circulating between us. I'm inviting you to let more of your energy flow.

Zacharie:
You mean because I don't express these feelings and don't use the words, I don't let the energy flow?

Anamika:
Yes, that's it.

Zacharie:
Sometimes I put up walls. But truthfully, I am hiding behind them. If I dared to go through the wall, I might feel better.

Anamika:
When you open up like this, I want to kiss you.

Zacharie:
Pareil pour moi. Same for me. Oh! There I said what I'm feeling! Phew...that's a relief... maybe now I will dare more. I might be very daring if I were with you physically.

Anamika:
Well, since we're not, we can connect with our words, our emotions and our energy.

Zacharie:
All of a sudden, I can feel your energy so strongly. What happened?

Anamika:
You let down your wall. That feels so good to me too and I feel so much energy moving as well.

Zacharie:
C'est si bon! It's so good, like rivers of honey flowing through my body. It's so delicious that I am having trouble concentrating on anything else. In this honey, *je suis fou*, I am crazy, but in a good way. In English you say, "over and over again" and "more and more." That's what I want!

Anamika:
When we connect like this, I feel so alive. This is what I want with you, over and over again, and more and more too!

Zacharie:
It's the same for me. I want to be with you

now so much. I imagine if we were together, *ce serait le paradis!* It would be paradise!

Anamika:
We <u>are</u> together. I know it's not physical, but it's just as strong and real. Can you feel my body as if I were there with you physically?

Zacharie:
Yes, I can feel it! *C'est magique!* This is magic! Your skin feels so soft and warm. I'm vibrating all over! It's miraculous!

Anamika:
I am drawing your energy into me. You are so delicious!

Zacharie:
I'm dancing inside you. Our rhythm is soft, but so strong. *C'est si bon.* It's so good. I feel like I'm home.

Anamika:
Yes, you're not only feeling me but also your true home inside of you!

Zacharie:
I don't want to move because it feels too good when we're connecting like this.

Anamika:
Endless waves and ripples of light are exploding and dancing in me.

Zacharie:
C'est extraordinaire! Magnifique! It's extraordinary! Magnificent!

It was extraordinary indeed. While I had experienced this kind of ecstatic energy exchange many times before, this was stronger and even more intimate.

The next day, as soon as we connected on Skype, we opened up into the euphoric energy again. His rivers of honey sent shivers of pleasure through my whole body.

Zacharie:
J'aime tout de toi. I love everything about you. I love breathing in your scent.

Anamika:
Can you feel me touching you with my etheric hands?

Zacharie:
Oui! Yes! I can feel your hands on my body and I can tell exactly where you're touching me. I'm sure you can feel my desire now.

Anamika:
Oh! Is your sexual desire the thing that you've been hiding?

Zacharie:
Oui. Yes. Now I have no more secrets from you. I feel you with me completely and I am with you in a field of love that goes on and on forever. It's infinite.

Anamika:
I love being in the infinite with you.

What was happening between us was feeling more and more like what I had wanted with him. I knew I didn't want a relationship that might end up needy, routine, controlling, self-sacrificing, or possessive. I didn't want anything I had ever experienced before.

I wanted a quality of relating that is an ongoing exploration and discovery, compassionate and free; a way of interrelating that expresses the personal and the infinite simultaneously.

I was finally experiencing what I wanted with him, but true to form, the more he opened up, the more I began to resist. Instead of staying present to what was beautiful between us, I found myself closing down.

Zacharie:
Do you want to swim in the rivers of honey with me tonight?

Anamika:
I'm in such a bad mood, I can't feel a thing.

Zacharie:
Don't worry. *Je t'aime comme tu es.* I love you as you are.

I was the one who had encouraged him to open up, and when he did, I stopped being open. What was my problem? I tried to explain my strange behavior to both of us…

✉

Dear Zacharie,

You are so honest and full of integrity. You share yourself with me freely. What a beautiful man you are!

I'm tired of pushing away. I want to work through this. My problem seems to be that I keep telling myself the story that you are not "The One." But before you feel rejected by that, understand that I have never succeeded in finding "The One."

What's beginning to dawn on me is that I am chasing an image that doesn't actually exist. What if there is no such thing as "The One?" This possibility is a crushing blow to the part of me that still longs for the perfect man. Maybe the concept isn't real, but you are real, and how we relate with each other is real.

What I am discovering with you has to do with learning to love beyond definition or form. To me this means continuing to love you beyond any fantasy of us being together forever. It also means continuing to love you even though our relationship is not "everything." While I know intellectually that no relationship is everything, I've been unconsciously looking for a person who would be the perfect everything.

My romantic fantasies have only served to keep me separate. With you, I am learning how to love even though you don't look like or act like anything that I thought I wanted. What you and I share is, in fact, real love beyond form.

My limited mind has entrapped me in a prison. It's a destructive cycle in which I yearn for love, judge myself and others as not perfect enough, feel the agony of being separate, and experience painful emptiness. I don't want to do this anymore.

Somehow, you've accepted me even with this crazy cycle. I don't know where our exploration will lead us. It's a moment by moment discovery, and you're a wonderful companion on this journey.

Ma chère Anamika,

Thank you so much for sharing with me your soulful reflections. I still have trouble trusting the love, too. Instead of trusting, I keep looking for concrete solutions to my problems. That's my mental prison. I'm learning not to punish myself when I choose my familiar prison instead of freedom. You can't begin to know how much the love we share helps me personally. It's like a light that guides me in my life. I admit that you are more advanced on your path than I am, but I have not lost hope of following in your footsteps in pursuing my own path in life. Thank you for being the diamond that illuminates my existence.

Zacharie,

I appreciate the honesty of our email exchange today. I want to keep relating to you, not try to build a relation-ship. Ships sink.

When I focus on what I think I want, I project my expectations of perfection and manipulative demands onto you. Doing that kills our delicious connection, which is what I really want.

I'm glad we live at a distance now because if we lived closer, we might push away to try to stay "free," or hold on too tightly out of "need." Now, because we have to reach beyond time and space, we have found a whole new way of relating to each other.

I cherish our connection and want it to blossom. I love you so, so, so, so much.

CHAPTER 5

i miss you deadly

```
Z: I miss you deadly.
A: Deadly? That's utterly adorable, but we don't say that in English!
Z: Then I am deadly creative, and deadly modest too!
```

Zacharie:
I have been thinking about the possibility of us getting closer. Would you like to share a room with me in a mental hospital? We could have separate beds, or share the same bed… if you wish.

Anamika:
Is that a proposal? How completely unromantic! I thought you were a Frenchman! If you are inviting me into your insanity, I have enough of my own, thank you. My preference is to meet elsewhere, so I'll wait for a better proposal.

Zacharie:
How about in a prison?

Anamika:
You consider that more romantic? You'll have to get out of prison if you want to meet me.

Zacharie:
What I'd really like is to be alone with you on a desert island.

Anamika:
Give me the coordinates and I'm there.

Zacharie:
Tu ne peux pas te tromper. Suis la direction de mon cœur. You can't get lost. Go in the direction of my heart. But to be serious, I invited you into a mental hospital and prison because I want a physical relationship with you and it's making me feel insane and trapped.

Anamika:
What about Sabine? Even though you have an open relationship, I would feel responsible and guilty if Sabine got hurt in any way because of me.

Zacharie:
When it's time for me to make some changes in my life, it would be my choice. I would be responsible. You've made my life more beautiful, so you don't have to feel guilty about anything.

I don't want to think about the future right now, because I don't know what to do. I trust that I'll know when it's time.

A: Here's your morning wake up text hug, cutie pie.
Z: *Bonjour ma chérie*. Your hug is such a nice way to be waken up.
A: to be woken up.
Z: I hate this verb!

Interestingly, he was always having trouble with the verb "to awaken." Yet, he was definitely awakening in his consciousness. I amused myself with the thought that he might conjugate this verb correctly when he chose to make deep changes in his life.

Zacharie:
I feel like I am in a trap, but it's a good trap

that brings me happiness. The first letter of my trap is "A" and the last letter is also "A." I don't have any desire to get out of this trap. I would like to stay trapped in this "AZA" trap.

Anamika:
This trap sounds better than your prison cell.

Zacharie:
Yes! Now that it's so much easier for me to express my feelings in words, I want to tell you that I feel ready to go further with you on this adventure.

Anamika:
That makes me so happy!

Zacharie:
When we connect in the energy my personal boundaries get blurred. *C'est comme si nous respirions le même air.* It's as if we're breathing the same air. It's as if we're one heart beating. I feel like I'm in the ocean of love and I am one with that ocean.

Anamika:
We are the infinite ocean of love itself.

Zacharie:
The Mathematician Georg Cantor proved there is infinity within infinity within infinity, and that infinity never ends.

Anamika:
That's so beautiful. I've never appreciated Math until this moment. The infinite is the true language we share.

Zacharie:
The reason I love science is that it opens a doorway into another world that is the true language of my soul. You look so beautiful right now, I don't want to speak. *Je veux seulement te regarder.* I just want to look at you…

I love how you look right now, just your natural self. When you're vulnerable like this, your skin looks like the skin of a baby.

Anamika:
Maybe it's the lamp light.

Zacharie:
Non, c'est toi qui est belle. No, it's you who are beautiful.

Anamika:
I feel so safe to be vulnerable with you as I sense your warm arms around me.

Zacharie:
C'est si délicieux. It's so delicious. I want to be with you physically so much.

Anamika:
I do too. And I miss you deadly.

Zacharie:
I'd like to sleep the whole night in your arms.

Anamika:
Me too, in fact the first thing I learned in French was *Voulez-vous coucher avec moi?* Do you want to sleep with me?

Zacharie:
In French, that means something more than just sleeping!

In fact, we were able to connect so intensely, we could sleep in each other's arms all night. It was extraordinary. We dreamed of the other during the night and discovered that we had shared the same dream.

As much as I was craving to go deeper into our ecstatic connection, I couldn't imagine actually physically making love with this man. It was safe to explore with him as long as we never met for real. At the end of one of our intense energy connections, my mood suddenly shifted and I found myself pushing him away again. I became morose and rejecting. He was visibly shaken by my sudden mood swing, and we didn't have time to talk it through before he had to go to bed.

My dear Zacharie,
I'm so sorry we didn't have time to talk earlier. I don't like the thought of you going to bed worried. That doesn't make for a good night's sleep. I feel shaken up about my sudden shift in mood. I hope we can talk soon. Big hug.

✉

Ma chère Anamika,

I had a lot of difficulty in handling the sudden change in your mood last night. It was so unexpected. I don't blame you because I know that you always have a good reason when you feel things.

Simply, it's very difficult for me to come back down to earth when I reach the level of bliss we were in last night. I hope that we can get past this quickly because I hate to think that your day would be full of sadness.

Je t'embrasse tendrement. I hug you tenderly,

Zacharie

I was so angry at myself for ruining his experience. Surprisingly, his response was not at all what I expected. Instead of blaming me, he showed tender concern for my wellbeing. Even though I was punishing myself, he managed to open my heart. I was relieved and grateful.

At the same time, Zacharie was also going through his own daunting challenges.

Zacharie:
This is not an easy period for me right now because I feel so strongly that I want to change my life. It's not just my relationship, it's also my work.

Teaching used to please me a lot, but these days, most of the students don't want to learn. They're there because they have to take my class to graduate from the university. I want teaching and learning to be like what we're doing together. Having said that, I don't know how to bring what we have into my work.

Our relationship is complex and interesting. It's unique for me. We don't know each other except through the Internet. We have never met in real life. Yet, our connection is so strong. The scientist in me wants to qualify exactly what this is. But, I don't have a name for it. I just know it's so important to me.

Yesterday, we didn't get to communicate and I didn't know if all was well with you. I was surprised how much that upset me. One can qualify that as love. But what we have is different than ordinary love and I have never felt anything like this with anyone before.

With Sabine, we spent almost one year as friends before becoming a couple. In the beginning we laughed a lot, but it soon became heavy and full of drama.

With you it's not complicated. Even though there are challenges, everything resolves so easily and we grow together.

Anamika:
The difference is when there's honest communication with compassion, it allows us to continue to grow. Could you bring what we are learning together into your relationship with Sabine?

Zacharie:
It's difficult because we've always been very intellectual and not emotional with each other. But when I'm with you, we resonate together. It's like making love.

Anamika:
That's really beautiful. How would you say that to me in French?

Zacharie:
Faire l'amour means to make love. When we use the word "sex," we are talking about the

act of sex. It's not romantic. If you say to have a sexual relationship, it's *une relation sexuelle.* That's a bit clinical or technical.

Anamika:
What is the most romantic way to say it?

Zacharie:
I don't know, but you could say, *"J'ai envie de faire l'amour avec toi."* I want to make love with you.

Anamika:
And what do you prefer?

Zacharie:
I prefer not to say it. I prefer to express my desires with my behavior. But come to think of it, I don't remember ever asking a woman to make love with me.

Anamika:
Really?

Zacharie:
You're the first.

Anamika:
You asked me? When?

Zacharie:
Just now.

Anamika:
Oh, very tricky! As an exercise for my French lesson?

Zacharie:
Oui! For my English lesson, how would you say it?

Anamika:
How would you say it in English?

Zacharie:
In a movie I once heard, "I want to have a baby with you."

Anamika:
Oh my God! Don't ever say that to a woman in English unless you mean it!

Zacharie:
Okay, two babies.

Anamika:
All right crazy professor, no babies for me, thank you.

Zacharie:
What if we were to meet each other for real and make love? We might both be disappointed or we might find out that we're even more compatible.

Anamika:
I don't know, but in either case, our relationship would change.

Zacharie:
From my experience, when you stay in a relationship without growing, it dies. But if I made a radical decision to meet you in person, I'm afraid I would do something irreparable to my relationship with Sabine.

Anamika:
That's one of the reasons it's so important to go slowly. As you open to more internal freedom, it might bring you into a deeper connection with Sabine, or a more peacefully disengaged relationship. Changing internally is what leads to a different external life as well.

You're changing very quickly these days. I'm watching you breaking free of your mental prison and risking your heart. This is your real freedom.

You don't have to know in advance how your life will look. You don't need to control the form. There's such richness in the unfolding. Can you trust that whatever new forms emerge will be wonderful and ever more liberating?

Zacharie:
Does this mean that as I evolve inside myself, it will be better for everybody around me?

Anamika:
Yes. Whether you stay together or separate, if you're freer and full of love inside, your relationship with Sabine will change for the better.

Zacharie:
I know you're right, but I'm afraid.

Anamika:
Fear is a natural part of the process of change. Let yourself gently feel it. If you had no fear, you wouldn't need courage. And it's taking a lot of courage for both of us to continue to explore greater intimacy outside of a conventional commitment.

I love that the English word "courage" is related to *cœur*, the French word for heart. What we're doing takes a lot of heart.

Speaking of fear, the new direction of our conversation scared me too. He was talking about getting together in person, which meant the possibility of a "real" relationship. I didn't want him to leave Sabine for me because as much as I loved him, I didn't have a clue what I wanted. Part of me was secretly hoping that he and Sabine would renew their relationship so I wouldn't have to make a choice.

Anamika:
Are you saying that you'd actually like to meet in person?

Zacharie:
Yes, I realized the truth of this tonight.

Anamika:
Thank you for telling me, but I am very surprised.

Zacharie:
You said from the beginning that you sensed I was not comfortable in my relationship.

Anamika:
Yes, but I respect your commitment to that relationship. I know you feel very connected to me, but I didn't know your feelings had become romantic.

I was surprised to learn that you and Sabine no longer have a sexual relationship but I assumed you still had romantic feelings for her because you're still with her.

Zacharie:
For me, friendship is the bedrock of everything and Sabine and I are still good friends. But, I'm becoming more aware of what's missing with her - a whole connection. I'm confused.

Anamika:
Maybe that's why I get mixed messages from you. I didn't know if you were hiding romantic feelings for me, or if you just didn't have them. And I still don't know exactly.

Zacharie:
I thought my feelings were obvious.

Anamika:
I don't know how you really feel unless you spell it out.

Zacharie:
Several times you asked me about my feelings. Every time, I tried to avoid the question, but not because I wanted to hide something from you. I wanted to hide something from myself.

For me, it's difficult to understand my own feelings. I am not used to thinking about them or sharing them. Maybe I'm afraid to know them.

Anamika:
Are you afraid to know them because it could result in great upheaval in your life?

Zacharie:
Yes, you're right one more time, number 567. I am afraid of my deep feelings and my deep truth because I don't think I'm ready for so much change.

Anamika:
I totally understand that. When you speak in this way, I can feel your heart. I just want to

know your true feelings, no matter what they are. Sharing this level of truth brings us closer.

Zacharie:
Wow, what an evening this has been!

CHAPTER 6

he prefers curves

The next level of our exploration took us into a whole new area. We began to recognize our deep cultural differences and the way our languages influenced emotional expression. This is where my French lessons became exciting and rich in an entirely new way.

Zacharie:
Maybe I am afraid of going deeper with you because my relationship with Sabine is very convenient for me. I have a big house with my own bedroom and office and so does she. We meet for dinner and share companionship and interesting conversation. This arrangement is comfortable, but it's not alive. However, the more I experience true aliveness, the more I realize I'm fooling myself wanting things to stay the same.

If I leave Sabine, my biggest fear is being alone. You're over there and I'm over here. If and when you meet "The One," what happens to me? I want you to be happy and free, but I am afraid there would be nothing left between us. It would make me very sad if you lost your desire to speak French.

Maybe we could still stay friends, but I am afraid of investing too much because I am afraid that I will want too much. I don't want to hope for a relationship with you that couldn't continue as intensely.

But most of all I can't hope to be with you. You are so advanced and wise. I know I'm not enough for you.

He became very quiet. He had just revealed all of his fears and looked very vulnerable. I anticipated the worst, that he would end our relationship.

Zacharie:
But, despite all those fears, I want to find the courage to really break free. The fact that I met you showed me that something is missing in my life. What's happening inside of me is unstoppable. I don't know what I'm go-

ing to do. But I can't imagine living this way much longer.

Anamika:
Zacharie, I understand your fears. My life also really began to change after we met. The way we relate has been a catalyst for both of us and we're in a beautiful and vulnerable process. What matters most to me is the unfolding, not the ultimate form our relationship takes.

Your decision about Sabine really has nothing to do with us. It's not about moving from one person to the next. It's about your own internal awakening and freedom.

Even if you were not with Sabine, I don't want to define our relationship. I love us growing the way we are.

Zacharie:
I appreciate your honesty and that's one of the things I treasure.

This conversation was illuminating. When I was talking about the new possibilities in his life, it was exciting. When it was about me getting closer to him, I felt like distancing myself and closing off my heart. My fears of entrapment arose, like with my mother, who was both dominating and needy. In our co-dependence, I felt squashed and drained. I had to distance myself to work it through with her.

By the time Zacharie and I spoke again, I was safely behind my wall of protection.

Zacharie:
You look so sad right now. Did I hurt you in some way?

Anamika:
No, you didn't hurt me. I'm hurting because I closed my heart.

Zacharie:
Sometimes I think it's my fault.

Anamika:
When I think it's my fault, I punish and blame myself. That's so painful.

Zacharie:
I've always felt it was up to me to be perfect

and get it right. So, when I didn't, I blamed myself.

Anamika:
When I do misguided things, it's an unsuccessful attempt to get my needs met. That's forgivable.

Zacharie:
I've never thought about it that way.

Anamika:
We both have a real need for love. When we fear being alone, we try to fill that need through someone else. Looking outside of ourselves becomes an addiction. In the past, my attempt to get love from someone else was like trying to fill a hole inside of me. I needed to get my "fix" over and over again.

The hole was the belief that I was unlovable and separate from the true source of love. What I've discovered is that my need for love gets met when I open my own heart. When my own love flows there is no hole, and then I can receive yours as well.

Zacharie:
You are very wise about this. Where did you learn all of these things?

Anamika:
From my own life experience. Like you in Physics, I'm also an explorer. My passion has always been to pioneer relating with myself and others and create new maps.

Zacharie:
I love being on this journey of exploration with you.

Anamika:
Me too. Exploration means not knowing what's ahead. That's scary and exciting. What I do know is that there is something beautiful opening between us. If we superimpose an old model of relationship on our exploration, what is there to discover?

Zacharie:
Cela demande un grand courage. That takes great courage. But, I really want to know what's going to happen.

Anamika:
I totally understand, because sometimes I

do too. But I also recognize that the desire to know is an attempt to be in control of life. We're taught to believe that being in control is how to get our needs met. But, life flows so much more elegantly when I relinquish control. Then my needs get met in more effortless and fulfilling ways. All I know is that what is occurring right now between us is magnificent.

Zacharie:
Okay, so our journey of exploration requires the courage to relinquish control. I wonder if I can do that?

Anamika:
It takes courage to speak another language, too. Compared to where we were in the beginning with our language skills, look where we are today. It would be fun to listen to some of our early audio recordings. They would really make us laugh now.

Zacharie:
I remember us both making a lot of mistakes, but I remember how passionate we were about learning. That was pretty courageous, wasn't it?

Anamika:
Yes, it was. Now, we can understand each other perfectly even when there are words we don't know because we understand each other through resonance.

Zacharie:
Yes, because of the flow of energy between us, I can understand you in a way that I can't understand anybody else in any language.

While our energy connections were deepening, so was our frustration at being locked inside of our computer monitors with more than 5,000 miles between us. While the energy connection was glorious, we were wanting more than 2D Skype. We both wanted to get closer.

Zacharie:
Here is your next lesson in French. Let's say we spent a wonderful day together. I would like to spend the night with you, but I don't want to be explicit. I'd rather be coy. So instead, I'd say, *Je ne veux pas te faire un dessin.* That roughly means, "I am not going to draw you a map."

Anamika:
It sounds like a much better proposal than the mental hospital, but it means I have to guess what you want. I know you're French, but would you willing to be direct with me tonight?

Zacharie:
I know you're American and always prefer I say it directly. But, in Physics a straight line is actually curved. Although a "straight" line is certainly the shortest, it's not the most romantic. I prefer curves.

Anamika:
In that case, you can be very curvy while you are talking straight to me.

Zacharie:
I see I'm not going to get out of this one. You know what I want to say.

Anamika:
I don't know exactly. I need to hear it and maybe you need to say it. In English, you can begin with, "I would like to...."

Zacharie:
I would like to...

Anamika:
...and you know that I prefer hearing it in French. Everything sounds better in French!

Zacharie:
Because it's more curvy in French? Okay, here I go. *Je veux te serrer dans mes bras.* I would like to take you in my arms. I feel very close to you emotionally and I have a desire to be close to you physically too.

Anamika:
Wow, I could feel what you said go all the way through my body. That felt amazing! When you say it that directly, what do you feel?

Zacharie:
A lot of happiness and also some frustration that it's not real right now. I would like it to be for real.

Anamika:
Me too. Did your feelings get stronger when you said it directly?

Zacharie:
When I speak my feelings, I can actually feel

them. This is new and exciting! Can you put your hand against mine on the screen?

Anamika:
I wish I could reach through the screen. It's so frustrating not to be able to touch you. When you're this present with your emotions, they transmit so strongly to me. I can feel what you are saying in my body.

Zacharie:
Learning this new language of resonance is the same process as learning English. In the beginning, I had to think about how to formulate my sentences. Now, English and feelings are both coming a little more easily. That feels good.

Anamika:
It's the same for me when I speak French. In French I access a softer part of myself. I've been waiting my whole life to get to know this tenderness.

When I speak French, the shape of my mouth, tongue and lips changes. It causes a different part of my brain's neuronal network to fire, which changes my way of relating.

Zacharie:
I notice that in English, I can be more direct.

Anamika:
And in French I can be more curvy.

Zacharie:
I'm a bit afraid of what is happening to me. More and more, it is not only that I want to speak with you, but I find that I need to speak with you. When I can't, I don't feel so good. This scares me a lot. I'm going to be direct. *Je veux être plus proche de toi.* I want to be closer to you. I want to meet you and be in the same room with you.

Anamika:
When you say "closer," what does that mean for you?

Zacharie:
I want to meet you for real and see if something will happen because our relationship is strange for me only by Internet.

Je veux te toucher et respirer ton odeur. I want to touch you and smell you. Something is missing, both in my life and in our relationship, too.

Anamika:
What is missing?

Zacharie:
If I were near you and you felt sad, I could hug you. I can't do that on the Internet. What if your Internet went down in a storm? Then we couldn't connect. That would be the end of us. Our relationship is so deep, but it's virtual.

Anamika:
Our relationship has touched our hearts and maybe your heart is wanting more.

Zacharie:
Yes, you are right, number 584 times of being right. *Mon cœur en veut davantage.* My heart is wanting more.

Anamika:
What more does your heart want?

Zacharie:
It wants to feel touched very deeply. Maybe it wants to feel love, a pure love.

Anamika:
That's beautiful. When we speak from our

hearts, it touches us deeply. Can you speak the words of your heart now?

Zacharie:
You want me to say the words?

Anamika:
Yes, because they will resonate in your heart. Say it in French if you prefer. That's the language of your emotions.

Zacharie:
J'ai peur de dire ce que j'ai sur le cœur. I'm afraid to speak my heart, because if I admit what I feel, I will have to change my life. It's so risky.

Anamika:
If you risk expressing what's in your heart, the pressure and tension that you're experiencing right now will melt away. You don't have to change your life just because you tell me what's in your heart.

Zacharie:
Okay…deep breath, here I go. *Je t'aime.* I love you. There. I said it!

Anamika:
And I love you!

Zacharie:
But I don't mean this in an ordinary way. I haven't wanted to call this love because it's something new for me. It's not the same as the love I've known before. If I were with you now, I would put my arms around you and then you would know how I feel.

Anamika:
When you speak from your heart, I know exactly what you mean. The problematic distance for you is not the Atlantic Ocean. It's the distance between your head and your heart. When you're in your heart there's no distance, no separation. The feeling of separation comes when you're in your head. Real love exists beyond the bounds of space and time.

Zacharie:
Oui, je t'aime tant, infiniment et pour toujours. Yes, I love you so much, infinitely and forever.

Anamika:
You have a beautiful, tender heart that's so pure. You're able to access it so easily.

Zacharie:
This feeling is like a different reality, not like the real world. I want to stay in this new reality with you, always.

Anamika:
This heart resonance <u>is</u> the real world and it's who you really are. You can access your heart any time.

Zacharie:
This is not ordinary love. It seems so vast and words can never express this infinite love.

CHAPTER 7

in the dance with you

I started feeling that there was an imbalance in our relationship. It seemed that I was the teacher or mentor with the answers and he was the student with the questions. I realized I was using my teacher mode to distance myself from the vulnerability of not being in control. I decided to risk receiving. Around this time, Shaqqara came down with her third bout of pneumonia in six months. She is 13 and has been my precious companion. I was afraid for her life and couldn't bear the thought of losing her. Usually I would suppress my fears, become a warrior, and handle it all myself.

Zacharie stepped in, in a way he had never done before to hold and protect me and Shaqqara. He wanted to be with us through the whole episode and I let him.

Anamika:
I just left Shaqqara in the hospital. She needs

to stay there for a few days and receive antibiotics intravenously. When I turned to go, she looked at me with so much sadness in her eyes. It tore my heart apart to leave her there. I can't stop crying.

Zacharie:
Just go ahead and cry. *Je suis avec toi, mon bébé*. I am with you, my baby. I'm putting my arms around both of you and holding you and Shaqqara safe in my heart.

Receiving felt so good, that even as Shaqqara was recovering, I let myself continue to welcome his strength.

Anamika:
As you were speaking in French right now, your strength as a man was really present in a very confident, but tender way. It was exciting and thrilling, even breathtaking. It's the part of you I have been waiting for.

Zacharie:
When I speak in French, I'm more secure. What I noticed today is when you spoke in

French, I felt your vulnerability. It's something I don't usually feel with you. Was it the French? Or are you starting to show me more of your vulnerability?

Anamika:
I felt so vulnerable with what was going on with Shaqqara and it felt so good to receive your strength.

Zacharie:
I have not seen that soft part of you before. You have been a kind of mentor to me, and I know that other people respect you greatly. And somehow, I couldn't connect with you as an equal.

Anamika:
I'm becoming acutely aware of how I have kept men at a distance.

Zacharie:
When Shaqqara was sick and you showed me your vulnerability, it made you seem more real to me. You don't have to stay in control and you don't have to be perfect with me.

Anamika:
Oh! I feel something breaking open inside of me! I am shaking with fear and excitement, laughing and crying at the same time. I am letting you in more deeply than I have let any man in before. As you find your strength and I allow my vulnerability, there's a new and rich dynamic between us.

As you know, I tend to hold the space for others. You are holding the space for me right now, with so much strength. I haven't allowed you to do this for me before. I haven't shared with you the places where I feel small and frightened. It feels so healing to share this with you now.

Zacharie:
It's very special for me, too. It's so gratifying to be this kind of man for you.

Anamika:
In my life, it's been easy to be a good mommy for men's hurt little boys. I'm sure there have been times when you've been a good daddy to women's hurt little girls. But this is different. During Shaqqara's illness, I expressed vulnerability as a woman, and was able to receive from you as a man.

It's like an entwinement of soul and spirit creating something completely new. This is like a dance of the masculine and feminine in their fullness. I feel such joy!

Zacharie:
I'm in this dance with you.

Zacharie:
What are you feeling after our last exchange?

Anamika:
Something very different. I have spent my life wanting, yearning and longing because I wasn't actually receiving. Now, instead of longing and yearning for you, I am actually experiencing you.

Zacharie:
Oui, c'est magique. Yes, it's magic. It's like being so deep inside of you that I know exactly what you are going to say before you say it.

Anamika:
What do you sense I am going to say?

Zacharie:

I love you.

Z: I am quite awaked and ready for a phone call. *Je pense à toi*. I am thinking of you.

A: I am quite awake.☺ I fell asleep last night to the sound of your voice in the audio file you made describing your day. I breathed in your words; you are breathtaking. I listen to your recordings again and again to master French. I began to learn French because it was the language of the heart, but now I want to speak fluently because it's where your heart most resides.

Z: There is nothing real but this love, and I love you in a way I couldn't have imagined before. I'm falling in two ways, in love and asleep. Have a good day beloved light of my life.

CHAPTER 8

excited as a flea

One of the big hurdles that Zacharie faced was taking his English exam. If he passed, it would qualify him to teach Physics at a prestigious university in England. He was certain that he wouldn't pass the exam.

Daring to try was a big challenge because of his harsh English teacher. He wanted to master English, but had no real confidence in his ability to do so.

He talked about going to England for an immersion course before the exam. Our language skills had always been in phase, like our relationship, and I was afraid that his English would become far better than my French. I didn't want us to get out of phase on any level, so I toyed with the idea of going to Paris for a French immersion course.

One morning, I woke up with an urgent desire to go to Paris. I tried to convince myself that my desire was more about taking the immersion course than about meeting Zacharie.

After much deliberation, I decided to go to Paris. When I told Zacharie, he freaked out and so did I. What did we think we were doing? We were actually going to meet!

Then he decided that the fear of meeting was preferable to missing each other if I was in Paris while he was in England. So he changed his plans. Instead of going to England, he would take his English course in Paris. I would go to French school and he would go to English school. We set a date for eight weeks away.

His English exam was scheduled for after our Parisian rendezvous. But out of the blue, he was notified that the date of his exam had been moved up. This was ideal, because he would be free of the worry of the exam and far more relaxed when we were together.

Prior to the trip to Paris, we spent a month speaking only English to help him prepare for his exam. We agreed that after his exam we would speak only French to help improve my language skills.

Eight weeks became seven.

Anamika:
Are you planning to stay home with Sabine and commute into Paris?

Zacharie:
No, I'm going to book a hotel for us.

Anamika:
With two separate rooms?

Zacharie:
Mais, bien sûr! But of course!

Anamika:
I'm surprised.

Zacharie:
I need my own space.

Anamika:
That's fine with me. Are you planning to tell Sabine that we're meeting in Paris?

Zacharie:
Don't worry, I'll handle it. That's my responsibility.

Anamika:
I won't feel comfortable if you're not clear with Sabine.

Zacharie:
I understand. I'm nervous about us meeting because we don't really know each other. What if we don't get along?

Anamika:
You already know the most important things about me.

Zacharie:
That's true. And you know a lot of things about me, things that I have never told anyone.

Anamika:
I don't know your body. But, I know your soul. I know your spirit. These are the important things.

Zacharie:
You know my voice, my appearance, and my face.

Anamika:
And your clothes…but only your sweaters. I

have never seen your pants or your shoes because they are under your desk.

Zacharie:
I can show you my shoes right now if you want. I'll lift my foot up to the monitor.

Anamika:
Oh, I like your shoes!

Zacharie:
Now my shoes won't be a surprise.

Seven weeks became six. The time was drawing nearer for our trip and his English exam.

Zacharie:
I am nervous about the exam. I would feel more confident if I had a speech prepared in English. I'd like to discuss Quantum Physics. Can you help me prepare it? If you recorded the speech, I could memorize it.

Anamika:
What would you like to say to begin your speech?

Zacharie:
"If I had made a speech a year ago about Quantum Physics, I would not have been able to say from experience how I affect my own reality. My study of English has proven these scientific principles…"

For the next month, we spoke only English. He listened to my recording of his speech every day. He was nervous and convinced he wouldn't pass. We talked about his fear of judgment by the examiners and that he believed he had to be perfect to be loved. I reminded him about what a courageous act taking this exam was for him, and that he was valuable regardless of the outcome.

When the day of the exam arrived, I woke up in the middle of the night to speak with him right before he went in. "This is just a test and doesn't determine who you are," I reminded him. "I know who you are and I love you just for you."

He promised to call me as soon as the exam was over. I went back to sleep. An hour later, a text came through.

Z: It's done! I was very stressing. I am sure I made many mistakes but I don't remember a thing that happened. I'm sure I didn't pass.

A: You were very <u>stressed</u> and it was very <u>stressful</u>?

Before I received an answer, the phone rang. It was Zacharie talking so fast in French, I could hardly understand a word he was saying.

What I heard is that there were three examiners and he felt like he was facing a firing squad. He was so terrified, he finished his ten-minute talk in five minutes. One of the examiners gently told him to slow down and breathe. This kindness was so different from his original English teacher that he was able to get through the exam!

```
A: When do you get the re-
sults?

Z: Not for a few months. I
don't want to think about it
anymore. Now I'm focusing on
meeting you.

A: I have my placement test
for French school and now I'm
the one feeling insecure.

Z: Your French is so much
better than you think and I
will be your professor as
always.
```

We turned our attention to preparations for our trip to Paris. Zacharie booked a very cheap hotel in Paris with two separate rooms. When I did some Internet research about this hotel, it turned out to be a real fleabag. I hoped this didn't reflect his overall style. I diplomatically proposed that we rent an apartment with two separate bedrooms so he could have his own space. Since I was scared about meeting him in person, getting separate rooms was sounding good to me as well.

A: I can't wait to meet you in person.

Z: I'm so excited and scared at the same time.

A: I've registered for French school.

Z: Congratulations! Now you are half in Paris. I am longing to meet you.

A: It's so strange to know you and not to know you at the same time!

Six weeks became two. I was nervous about my French, but more nervous about meeting him. Even though I saw our relationship in the light of growth, my adolescent fantasies were running rampant. I was imagining a passionate romantic tryst under the Eiffel Tower. It was as if Zacharie would miraculously become somebody else, "The One" of course! I wondered if my adolescent would ever grow up. Apparently not!

A: I took my oral exam yesterday by phone. I was so jittery, I told her, "*Je suis excitée comme une puce.*" I am as excited as a flea. It made her laugh.

Z: *C'est très idiomatique!* That's quite idiomatic! You remembered that one! Bravo!

A: I can't wait to be with you in person. I'm picturing us together walking down *Les Champs Elysées.*

Z: Our relationship is the most important thing in my life.

A: *Moi aussi.* For me too. You are a treasure.

Z: I am in bed and I feel you by my side.

A: You're such a crazy bull!

Z: Because you drive me crazy.

A: mmmmmmm...

Z: I think you have mis-spelled that word and left out an "m."

Two weeks became one day and I was beyond excited. I was walking Shaqqara on the road near my house. It was our daily routine. Suddenly, she stepped on a bee's nest. In an instant, she had bees all over her body, tangled in her long silky hair. Without thinking about getting stung, I bent down and frantically pulled the bees out of her hair. When I tried to stand up, my lower back went into spasm and I couldn't move. I practically crawled home.

My friend, a massage therapist, made a trip to my house but to no avail. The muscles were not going to let go and it was no better the next day. But, there was no way I was going to miss my trip to Paris.

A: I'm on my way to the plane, in a wheelchair. I feel like I've ruined our trip because I can't walk.

Z: *Je t'aime en toutes circonstances.* I love you under all circumstances.

A: You do me such good.

A: I am on the plane. I can't wait to be with you in person.

Z: *Tendres bisous.* Tender kisses.

A: Oops, plane taking off!

A: We've landed! *L'aventure commence!* The adventure begins!

Z: *Bienvenue, ma chérie.* Welcome, my sweetheart. How is your back?

A: A very charming Frenchman wheeled me straight through customs and out to the curb. I tentatively tried out my French: "*Est-ce que tous les hommes en France sont aussi gentils que toi?*" Are all French men as nice as you? He laughed and kissed me warmly goodbye on both cheeks.

Z: I wish I were kissing you too!

I took a taxi to the apartment we had rented. It was a cold rainy winter day in Paris. As we drove through the wet, bleak street, I thought to myself, "I left sunny Southern California for this?"

The taxi driver helped me upstairs with my luggage. The apartment was only a little better than the fleabag hotel. It was small and basic, and completely lacking in coziness. More importantly, there was only one bedroom, with a sofa bed in the living room. I lowered myself carefully onto the only chair. My back was in agony. I felt utterly disappointed and wanted to go home.

Zacharie was not scheduled to arrive until two days later. That first night on my own I started to feel really sick, with bone-rattling chills. I began to cough and was unable to breathe. *Quelle drôle d'aventure!* Some adventure!

A: Slept 12 hours. Feel terrible. Can't wait to see you.

Z: I'm on the train to Paris. I'll be there in 30 minutes.

Then what seemed like hours later I got another text:

> **Z:** I'm in the cab. What is the room number?

As he was climbing the stairs, I was feeling deathly ill and suddenly dreading his knock on the door. I was sure that I wouldn't find him attractive and my romantic fantasies would be dashed. I was panicking, trapped, sick and in a foreign country unable to walk.

He was getting more and more excited.

> **Z:** I'm walking towards the door.

Then came the dreaded knock at the door. I considered not opening it and jumping out of the window. I don't remember walking to the door. But, I do remember my first reaction when I opened it.

CHAPTER 9

paris, city of romance?

I opened the door. There he was. My heart flew open with love. Then just as quickly, I noticed several long hairs sticking out of his eyebrows. I knew for certain he was not "The One."

I had flown over 5,000 miles to find out if there was any chance he was "The One." Now, there was no further doubt. I crumbled inside and wanted to die right there in the doorway.

Zacharie, on the other hand, was elated. He wrapped me in a big bear hug and said, "This is so much better than Skype!" Then he kissed me on the lips. His kiss was warm and tender, just like when he came to me in the "dream" last summer. But I was stiff and tense.

His arms were still around me and he said, "Oh, I love your clothing, it's so soft." I closed my eyes and listened to him speaking in French. It was like music, reminding me of why I had come. In the same instant, I was certain coming to Paris was a mistake. And oh, no, we were sharing an apartment!

My head was spinning. The fever was so strong by then that I had to go lie down. I left him standing in the doorway, indicating he could sleep on the sofa bed, and escaped to the bedroom. I was clearly running a high temperature, probably a bit delirious and needed to think. I lay gingerly on the double bed, which was actually two single mattresses crammed together. “Maybe I can check into a five star hotel,” I thought desperately, “and catch the first plane out in the morning.”

Suddenly, Zacharie appeared in the bedroom doorway with his suitcase. He came into the room, hung up his clothing, took off his shirt and jumped into bed next to me.

I was mortified. He was overweight, out of shape and had a strong body odor. I froze. “He wants to make love?” I thought to myself. It was my worst nightmare come true.

I told him delicately I felt too sick. He understood and gently got off the bed, disappearing into the bathroom. Alone in the room, I was shocked and dismayed at how freaked out I was. On the other hand, despite all of Zacharie's proclamations about needing space, why had he followed me into the bedroom? He had moved right in.

I grabbed my cell phone and called a friend in Colorado. I was in desperate need of advice. "What should I do?" I whispered urgently into the phone. "He smells bad and I want to go home."

She calmly suggested I ask him to take a shower. "But I've never had to ask a man to take a shower before," I complained. "I know," she replied gently. "All of your men have been physically fit, well groomed and clean. This must be a nightmare for you, but tell him to take a shower."

As he came back in the room, I quickly hung up the phone. "You must be tired," I suggested. "Maybe you would like to go and take a shower?" Thankfully, he complied. Listening to the water running I asked myself, "What's your problem? He's so gentle and accommodating." I couldn't stop coughing. I had a fever. I didn't know what to do.

When he came back into the bedroom, things did not get better. Unaware of my sensitivities to chemicals and strong smells, he had put on a pungent men's cologne. My back was in spasm, I couldn't breathe and suddenly the cologne was giving me a splitting headache.

I apologized profusely explaining my sensitivity to smells and asked if he would go back in the shower to wash off the cologne. I was amazed at his accommodating response. He did take another shower, but to make matters worse, he had to repeat the process three more times to get the smell off of his skin to my satisfaction.

I was absolutely appalled by my behavior and by the whole situation. This was his first physical encounter with me. *Quel romantisme!* How utterly romantic! By now, I imagined that <u>he</u> probably wanted to go home. I was in hell. But Zacharie was in heaven.

After the third shower he sat on the edge of the bed in his towel and tenderly rubbed my hand. "It's so wonderful to be together physically, at last, isn't it?" He was so sweet and adorable, I couldn't bear to tell him how I really felt.

Much to my dismay, I found myself talking about a friend who taught men's grooming. "She teaches men about the importance of brushing your teeth and trimming your eyebrows..." When I heard that coming out of my mouth, I knew I had lost it entirely!

I suggested it was time to sleep, expecting he would go into the other room. Instead, he dropped his towel and crawled naked into bed beside me. When he came closer to my side to cuddle, he fell into the crack between the mattresses. We both had to laugh.

By the next afternoon my fever was so bad, I needed to see a doctor. Zacharie located one several blocks away. I was able to walk, but only very tentatively and with a great amount of pain. He took my arm, patiently guiding and supporting me along the cold, damp street.

When we arrived at the office, the doctor greeted us with a cigarette in his mouth. The office was thick with smoke. For someone from Southern California, the land of air filters and health foods, this was a shocking affront.

On top of this, I already couldn't breathe. Could things possibly get any worse? Even Zacharie was offended by the chain-smoking doctor. When I complained about the smoke, his assistant helpfully attempted to mask it by spraying the entire examining room with the most pungent, floral, chemical perfume I had ever smelled in my life. I wanted to die all over again.

Although it was the middle of winter, Zacharie suggested they open the windows to air out the room. It was a good idea, but didn't help. By now the room was freezing, and the smoke and perfume were exploding inside my head.

I asked if the doctor could examine me outside in the street. He thought I was crazy, but I insisted that the cold was more tolerable than the smells.

Sensing my distress, Zacharie suggested conducting the examination in the hallway. The doctor shrugged, "There's a first time for everything." The three of us made our way onto the landing. Zacharie shielded me from possible onlookers as I opened my down coat and pulled up my sweater so the doctor could listen to my lungs. He asked me if the mucous I was coughing up was yellow.

I said I wish it were, but unfortunately it's green. *"Oh, tu connais la différence?"* "Oh, you know the difference?" he asked.

We continued the examination in French, and by the end, the doctor and I were good friends. He prescribed antibiotics and handed me the prescription. I thanked him and on the way out I told him, *"Tu devrais arrêter de fumer."* You should stop smoking. After all I had put him through, I was surprised when he responded with a smile, *"Tu as raison. Je vais essayer de le faire."* You're right, and I'm going to try.

After a day on French antibiotics, the fever started to break. But I continued to cough up disgusting green mucous for many more days. It took the entire trip to recover from this bout of bronchitis.

The only good thing about the disgusting mucous was that it seemed a good excuse to keep Zacharie at bay in bed. He attributed my unexpected distant behavior to my illness, and was very patient. He wisely trusted that I would open up to him eventually. He conscientiously took a shower every morning and every night. Finally, I realized that if I was going to enjoy this trip, I had better just surrender and connect with him. So despite the ugly apartment, bad back, sickness, and terrible smells, I decided to relax and enjoy myself.

One evening, I was lying on the sofa and he took my feet in his hands and gently began to rub them. His hands were warm and healing. I was able to feel the person I had connected with so deeply on the Internet. I let myself remember his tenderness. When he said, “Being with you like this is enough for me,” in his rich resonant French, I was able to finally let go.

The next day, even though I was still terribly sick, I went to French immersion class. This was, after all, the ostensible reason for my trip to Paris. I hobbled up the steps and coughed through the whole class, but loved being there anyway.

Zacharie attended his English immersion course while I was taking French. Each day after school, we would meet back at the apartment. He bought colorful flowers, cooked a beautiful meal, and the apartment began to feel cozy and inviting.

I began to look forward to our time together, like my dog, Shaqqara did with her doggie friend,

Thor. We got into a rhythm of laughing together, learning language and enjoying each other's company. And like with Thor, despite myself, Zacharie seemed more appealing.

I became aware that it was my own expectations and judgments that made him seem imperfect. My belief that a man had to be perfect wasn't allowing me to simply open my heart.

Zacharie did a stellar job taking care of me while I was sick, but what was more surprising is that I let him. It was good for him to give and for me to receive.

I'm embarrassed to remember our next "French farce." My over sensitivity to smells came between us once again. One night Zacharie touched my face and I was repelled by the worst stench on his fingers I had ever encountered before. It smelled as if he had just stuck his fingers in dog poop and then put his hand on my face.

I recoiled. "What is that horrible smell?" In dismay, he sniffed his hand, but shrugged, "I don't smell anything." Having been through the doctor and cologne fiascoes, with great concern for my wellbeing he rushed to the bathroom to wash his hand. He came back and gently touched my face with his other hand. To my chagrin, it smelled the same if not worse. Suffice it to say, after many scrubbings we went to bed laughing about sensitivities and bad odors.

We fell into a pleasurable rhythm together. During the day we went to our separate language classes. We met at the apartment in the afternoon and then shopped for our meal. In the evening we laughed about the linguistic lunacies of the day. I said, "I used the word *'épouser'* to my French teacher," I told Zacharie, "instead of *'pousser'*." "You told him it was okay to marry you," Zacharie laughed, "instead of saying it was okay he had bumped into you."

The "French Farce" continued one evening at dinner. That afternoon I was in the market. I had been telling Zacharie about a particular kind of seaweed I eat in California. I wanted to share it with him but they didn't carry my brand. So, I bought what they had and added it to the beautiful soup he had made.

We sat down to enjoy the soup. It tasted like salty cardboard. My seaweed had entirely ruined his soup. We laughed until tears ran down our cheeks. As I looked across the table at this man, I realized what a safe, warm cocoon he was providing into which I could let go as I had never done before with a man. Some ancient tension was melting away inside of me. It was liberating as well as vulnerable. Zacharie was very gratified providing this safety and asked for nothing in return. He seemed to love being with me no matter what.

However, Zacharie would call Sabine every night. I was hesitant to ask what was going on because I wanted to respect his privacy. What kind of open relationship is this when there's so much secrecy involved? It felt awkward and uncomfortable to me.

One night, after a particularly romantic stroll through *Le Quartier Latin*, he suddenly wanted to talk about his relationship with Sabine. He confessed he was telephoning her every night out of guilt. He explained that over the 25 years they had been together, they had a very limited sexual relationship. She was inhibited sexually and he thought it was his fault.

He hadn't had much experience prior to meeting her and had never really enjoyed being touched. As a result, he concluded that sex must be over-rated and wasn't for him. Thus, he had retreated into his mind, living in his intellect, and ignoring his sexuality.

His confession was so full of sadness and loss, that when we got home, I began to stroke him tenderly. I could feel how sensitive his body actually was and how he was craving touch. I could feel him drinking in my touch just like he drank in our first energy session on Skype. All of his bodily senses came alive at once. For the first time he realized the utter deliciousness of being in his body and of his own sexuality.

As soon as his body opened up, he was able to be so much more present with me. Our time together turned into a luscious exchange of energy, sensuality and sexuality. Along with his awakening, I was surrendering more and more into the pleasure of being with him.

I wasn't expecting the depth of passion and strength he possessed. It opened spaces within me

I hadn't discovered before and created a warm and limitless ocean in which we dove and swam.

"Your body is so welcoming," Zacharie remarked. "I love everything: your smell, the texture of your skin, your warmth, and how you hold me in your arms. *C'est un délice, c'est le paradis.* The time we spend together is a delight, it's paradise."

I agreed. The pleasure of being together was so much more than I could have imagined. When we connected into the limitless energies we had shared on Skype, and then brought them into our bodies, lovemaking moved from the ordinary to the divine.

Infinite energy is inexhaustible and we could ride its waves together for hours. It recharged and reenergized our bodies and spirits. Rather than sightseeing, we chose to stay in this sublime state for the rest of our time together.

By the end of our time in Paris, we were in such a sweet harmony together, it was very sad to part. He took me to the *Montparnasse* train station. We stood on the platform holding each other's hands, not knowing if we would ever be together again. We both cried as my train pulled out of the station.

CHAPTER 10

earthquake in my heart

As the train pulled out of the station, I sat cradling my cell phone, hoping for a text. It came 5 minutes later.

Z: I am on the train heading home. I am completely crazy about you. My heart is so heavy, but when I think of you everything is lighter. I love as I have never done before.

A: You love with all of yourself, and your love is beautiful.

The trip home was filled with thoughts of Zacharie and our time in Paris. At the same time, I didn't know anything about what the future with him would bring. I had to choose again and again to stay present with our loving connection and let go of any potential outcome.

As soon as we landed at LAX, I turned on my phone, hoping there would be a text.

> **Z:** It's my first night back home. I am thinking of you and it makes me happy. All night I was imagining being in your arms. I miss your eyes, your smile, your voice, your hands caressing me, and all of you.
>
> **A:** I miss you so much, *mon bébé*, my baby.

I got home exhausted, but couldn't go to sleep without one more text.

> **A:** I'm so sad being away from you.
>
> **Z:** Same here, are you home now?

A: Yes, in bed, crying.

Z: *Je suis avec toi, mon bébé*. I am with you, my baby. It's normal to feel vulnerable because you are so open now after our trip together.

A: Your love is like a blanket that's so warm and soft.

Z: I miss you deadly.

A: You make me smile.

Z: I crave being in your arms.

A: My arms are around you I feel your delicious energy all through my body.

Z: I love you so much and when I think of you I go crazy.

As soon as I woke up the next morning we got on Skype. He looked despondent, just how I was feeling.

Zacharie:
I feel so empty without you. The contrast of what I felt in Paris and my life now is so apparent. Our time together was full of richness and pleasure, even the doctor and the seaweed.

Without you, I have the sense of being imprisoned in my own life. The nights with you were soft and sweet.

Anamika:
What happened with Sabine when you got home?

Zacharie:
I was going to speak honestly with Sabine about our relationship when I found out that she has to have surgery. It was very unexpected.

Anamika:
Is it anything serious?

Zacharie:
I hope not, but it's urgent. I really want to support her through this.

Zacharie:
Sabine had the surgery today and the test results came back negative, so she's going to be okay. I'm relieved, but I'm also aware that the time I'm spending with her is out of duty and obligation. I still care about what happens to her, but my feelings have changed.

If I keep procrastinating, it will prevent me from making the choices and decisions I really want to make. I have come such a long way and I see the difference between who I was and who I am now. The time that I spend with Sabine has a very different quality than my time with you. It's like two different worlds.

Anamika:
You need to speak with her, but take your time. When you make a pressured choice, it may not be the best one. You've lived together for 25 years. Redefining that can feel very threatening.

Zacharie:
We own our house together, but it's not the house that's important. It's who is going to keep the cats. My house feels like a prison because of the unresolved situation with Sabine. I've read your first book and I know that you've had to renounce things for your freedom.

Anamika:
Yes, many times.

Zacharie:
The choice I have to make is a lot simpler than what you went through.

Anamika:
You can't compare. For each of us, choosing freedom can be challenging. I think you are feeling the difference between the ease and joy you experienced in Paris and the pressure you are experiencing now. Are you punishing yourself for that?

Zacharie:
Oui, tu as raison, numéro 678. Yes, you are right, number 678.

Anamika:
I don't think your house and unresolved situation with Sabine are the prisons. It's your self-judgment that imprisons you. Can you be present with where you are in your process and appreciate each step of your journey? That will let you out of your prison and be at peace.

Zacharie:
I'm afraid of what I really want. In Paris, I felt so accepted by you that for the first time in my life, I was truly myself. I felt free.

Anamika:
Can you feel something very tight in your body right now?

Zacharie:
Yes, I feel tense in my stomach.

Anamika:
I feel like you want to cry right now.

Zacharie:
Oui, j'ai envie de pleurer. I do want to cry. In fact, this morning I watched all of your videos on your website again. I cried while watch-

ing them, not only because I miss you, but because of remembering our special time together. After seeing the videos, I felt very sensitive; the smallest things made me happy or sad.

Anamika:
I know, it's always such a relief when you let your energy flow. What are you feeling now?

Zacharie:
That I am so glad to be feeling again. When I feel, I am connected to my real self and I feel strong.

✉

Ma chère Anamika,

Since Paris I feel strong, like a new man with a new virility. As a result, our relationship is more equal. In the beginning, you were a sort of guide and mentor to me but I feel like we're helping each other now. It's also gratifying to know that you're a woman and it's just as simple as that.

I send you a ton of soft and passionate kisses.

My Zacharie,

I've always wanted to learn to sing, just like I wanted to speak French. I've been studying singing and it's so joyous for me, but I'm insecure about my singing just like I was about my French. I feel very vulnerable singing this to you, but I wanted to give you a special present for your birthday. Eventually I'd like to sing you something in French, but in the meantime here's a song in English. It's about an unusual relationship that touches the person's soul.

Anamika

Ma chérie,

C'est le plus beau cadeau que j'ai jamais reçu. This is the most beautiful gift I've ever received. The words and the way you sang it touched me.

I want to cover you with tender kisses, my sweetheart.

My Zacharie,

As I write this we just had a big earthquake that shook the whole house!!! An earthquake releases so much power. It reminds me of how potent your energy is. When you penetrate my heart, every cell of my body feels your power. It's like an earthquake in my heart.

CHAPTER 11

even his puns are sad

Zacharie was nervously awaiting the results of his English exam. He was scared of not passing, and of passing. Not passing would mean failure. Passing would mean the possibility of moving to England.

A: Did I wake you up with my email?

Z: Yes, but it's almost the best way to be waked up. I said "almost" because a kiss from you is certainly even better.

A: Here's a kiss. Don't for-get, woken up.☺

Z: Did you get my SMS about how sleeping is a waste of

time when I'm next to you because I prefer doing other things?

A: No, I didn't.☹

Z: I'm afraid I made a mistake.

A: Now you think that sleeping is more important?

Z: No, I think I sent the SMS to someone else!

A: To the President of your university?

Z: No, his wife!

A: She probably needs a crazy bull like you in her life!

Z: Maybe that will help me pass my exam.☺

Z: Too long without the sun. You, and the one in the sky. It's unfair I can't be with you now. It seems I have to wait one secular before being with you again.

A: One secular? You mean one century?

Z: Yes and I'm ready to eat 1kg of seaweed to be with you right now. *Je t'aime tant, je suis fou.* I love you so much, it drives me crazy.

A: mmmmmmmmm... No typo this time?

Z: This time you added an extra "m."

Z: I got the test results. I passed!

A: I'm so proud of you! You did it!!! Here's a big hug. I wish I were with you to celebrate.

Z: I had to go by our apartment on the way to the university. I'm happy about passing the exam but so sad not to share this special time with you.

A: *Moi aussi.* Me too. I'm glad we're speaking French right now because it brings me closer to our time in Paris. We've been speaking a lot of English recently. Your English is so good now.

Z: It's so good because we are speaking French!

Zacharie:
Even though I passed the exam and my future is more open, I can see that there are still prison walls in my life.

Anamika:
Like what?

Zacharie:
My attachment to Sabine feels like glue. It avoids me moving forward.

Anamika:
It <u>prevents</u> you from moving forward.

Zacharie:
And it prevents me from speaking good English too!
On a more serious note, I want to know real freedom in my life.

Anamika:
If you jump into the past or the future you will not have access to the limitless potential that the present holds.

Zacharie:
I'll try to avoid thinking about the future, but I like thinking about the past with you in it.

Z: I didn't sleep well last night. There was a storm outside and inside. My brain has been working too hard. Not enough connection with my feelings.

A: You've been trying to solve your life?

Z: Yes, instead of feeling. I am trying to prevent myself from feeling pain.

A: Are you making up scary stories about the future?

Z: Yes. That seems to be what's causing me pain. I don't want to live without the lightness we experience together.

A: That lightness still exists in you now, but it's not in your mind. It's in the flow of energy in your body.

Z: Okay, I'll meet you there.

Anamika:
You were with me all night in my dreams. We were entwined in a sea of love, melting into each other. It was breathtaking!

Zacharie:
I felt us together too. We were in an intoxicating dance of love. It was wonderful. But I really won't be satisfied until we are together again physically.

Z: I miss your body. But, I feel something strong and beautiful in my heart.

A: Like the sun warming you from the inside out?

Z: I can feel that! On second thought, no "can" needed. I should have said, I feel that; "can" is only for drinks.

A: Are you covering your emotions with a pun?

Z: Yes, even my puns are sad without you.

A: Oh, I see, it's your puns who are sad; it's not you!

.

Z: Good morning, my sweetie, I am gardening. It helps me feel better. I am trying not to think about how much longer I must wait until I see you again.

A: Is it working?

Z: No. Right now I am jealous of your excellent accent in French.

A: What? You want my American accent in French?

Z: No, your American accent in English.

A: Your charming French accent in English is what I adore!

Z: Okay, I'll keep my French accent. But, I really want your other qualities that make everyone fall in love with you.

A: I'm glad you appreciate me, but perhaps valuing yourself is what's needed now?

Z: Yes, you are right, number 858.

A: I guess the gardening worked after all!

Z: But you are the most beautiful flower in my life.

A: And you are the most romantic person I've ever met, and not only because you're French. It's because you're you.

CHAPTER 12

what about sabine?

In the time we were apart, Zacharie was beginning to think about the possibility of a new job in England after 25 years of teaching. He was also considering living in Paris without Sabine.

I was contemplating making my work more public. This was a big step after many years of working with people one on one and in small groups. After Paris, our lives were expanding.

We both began feeling the desire to get together again. My secret wish was to have him come to Malibu in the summer, but I didn't want to propose it. I had initiated the Paris adventure, and I felt that the next big step had to come from him when he was ready.

Zacharie:
What's Malibu like in the summer?

Anamika:
Why don't you come and find out?

Zacharie:
Are you inviting me?

Anamika:
Do you want to come?

Zacharie:
Do you want me to come?

Anamika:
I want you to come if you want to come.

Zacharie:
Okay, I want to come.

Anamika:
What about Sabine?

Zacharie:
Yesterday, I was ready to have a conversation with her and suddenly, there was a new problem. Each time I try to speak with her, some kind of issue arises. First, it was the surgery, and now it's a work related situation

that prevents us from speaking. What do you think this means?

Anamika:
It could be resistance to having this conversation.

Zacharie:
It feels like unconsciously she's aware that something is changing between us.

Anamika:
You're growing, and it's impossible for her not to feel that at some level.

Zacharie:
She doesn't spend much time with me. She travels a lot for her work. We have very separate lives.

Anamika:
That doesn't mean she's not sensing something. What exactly do you want your relationship with her to be?

Zacharie:
I don't know. Maybe I want to continue to live

with her as my friend, and be free to be with you too.

Anamika:
If she refuses?

Zacharie:
I'm ready to risk living alone.

Anamika:
If you're not content in the relationship the way it is, she probably isn't either. When you do what's right for you, it will be good for her as well. You will be liberating both of you.

Zacharie:
Theoretically, I understand what you're saying, but on a practical level I can't imagine she would be happy with this arrangement.

Anamika:
You can only do what's right for you.

Zacharie:
I've been doing that with English. I haven't read a book in French for months, only in English. Isn't that curious?

Anamika:
What does English mean to you?

Zacharie:
I thought English was just useful for my life, but it actually makes me happy.

Anamika:
When you are happy, it spills over into the rest of your life. I went to Paris because I love you and I love French. I don't <u>need</u> French, it just makes me happy. And while I was in Paris, all kinds of amazing things happened.

Zacharie:
Yes, like a backache, bronchitis, and bad odors. Tell me again, what was good for you in France?

Anamika:
I let myself become very open and vulnerable because you were there to hold me. I surrendered and received so much love that a new butterfly began to emerge inside of me.

Zacharie:
Listening to you, I've decided to come to Malibu.

Anamika:
What about Sabine?

Zacharie:
I've decided to speak to Sabine and nothing will get in the way. I plan to talk to her about the changes in my life. I won't be telling her about you because you are not the issue. I have never given myself permission to follow my heart and do what I want to do. If I don't, I'm not really giving myself permission to live. I can't try to second-guess her, or what's going to happen in the future. I have to be in the moment and trust what feels right now.

Anamika:
Bravo, I'm so excited! This is a big breakthrough and I can't wait to see you in Malibu!

Zacharie:
I tried to talk to Sabine but I didn't feel strong and brave enough.

I said, " I want to be free." She said, "You are free."

Anamika:
Did you explain to her what you meant by free?

Zacharie:
No, because her answer took me by surprise. There was nowhere else to go in the conversation. I don't think I have any illusions of being able to save our relationship, but I don't want to throw it all away, either.

Anamika:
What <u>do</u> you mean by free?

Zacharie:
I want a different kind of relationship with her. I no longer have romantic feelings for her, just a deep friendship.

Anamika:
And you were scared to tell her that?

Zacharie:
Yes. We have exhausted what we had. I can't find words that sound right to help her understand who I've become.

Anamika:
Maybe you're not really ready to come to Malibu this summer. It's okay to wait.

Zacharie:
There are so many challenges for me in coming to Malibu. Not only is it scary to talk to Sabine, but I've never travelled internationally before. I have to get a passport, buy a ticket, get a visa and many other difficulties like that.

Anamika:
After you resolve things with Sabine everything else will be easy.

Zacharie:
You're probably right. The contrast between the permission you give yourself to follow your heart and what I give myself is very evident. The fact that you said I didn't have to come this summer released the pressure and made me realize how much I do want to come. I'm going to speak to Sabine now.

Anamika:
Did you resolve things with Sabine?

Zacharie:
I should explain to you what Sabine meant when she said that I was free. A few years ago she met a man and became very close to him.

Anamika:
Close in what way?

Zacharie:
She would spend several days with him at a time. She still sees him.

Anamika:
What? Are you kidding! Then why is it such a big deal for you to have another relationship if she's already set the precedent? What kind of open relationship are you having if you're not telling her the truth?

Zacharie:
Our agreement was to not ask or tell about other relationships. Also, she assured me many times she would not leave me for him. Her new relationship really unsettled me, but she kept reassuring me that our relationship came first. But what I have with you is very different from what she has with him.

Anamika:
In what way? What is the nature of their relationship?

Zacharie:
I don't want to know, so I don't ask questions.

Anamika:
Then how do you know it's different if you don't know anything about it? Would it make a difference to you if they were having sex?

Zacharie:
She's not a very sexual person, so I assumed they weren't having a sexual relationship.

Anamika:
Why don't you want to know?

Zacharie:
I thought I couldn't live without her. So it's easier not to know.

Anamika:
What did you think you couldn't live without?

Zacharie:
I didn't feel confident enough by myself.

Anamika:
What need did you think she was fulfilling?

Zacharie:
Hmmm, let me think. Maybe safety and also companionship.

Anamika:
Do you still feel the need for that from her?

Zacharie:
I feel more confident now, but 25 years is a long time…

Anamika:
In Paris, there was an awkwardness between us because of your attachment to Sabine.

Zacharie:
I know. I wasn't ready to face it then, but now I must because I want us to be completely at ease in Malibu. The problem with Sabine and I has nothing to do with you. However, since being with you, I can't reassure her that she's my primary relationship. I have changed, and so have my wants and needs.

Anamika:
I'm glad you feel that way because I wouldn't want you to replace her with me. That would be like going from one dependency to another. What I respect about you is that you are finding your own strength and value. Only then can you make clear choices about relationships.

I think her relationship with this man was an indication that there has been the need for this kind of shift between the two of you for a long time.

Zacharie:
Looking back, everything shifted when she met that man. I met you because I was ready to grow. But it wasn't because of you. It was because of me.

Anamika:
Exactly. And there are infinite possibilities about how you and Sabine can move on together, but they all start with honesty with yourself and each other.

Zacharie:
I have made a lot of excuses for not really living. I have played a role in my work and

relationships. I tried to be the good teacher, the good son, and the good partner. I haven't been myself. I haven't been real. I don't want to be dead anymore. I want to feel alive. So, I'm going to talk to Sabine now.

Zacharie:
I spoke with Sabine again today. She asked if she would have a place in my new life. Like me, she was afraid of losing what we have.

Anamika:
What did you say?

Zacharie:
I told her that our friendship would never die. We'll keep whatever is real and we'll get rid of what doesn't work.

Anamika:
How did she feel about that?

Zacharie:
I think she already understood that something needed to change, but the words helped her.

Anamika:
You and Sabine are both good people. The problem is not you as people, but the old patterns between you.

Zacharie:
I've started breaking my dependence on her. I told her she would have to make her own decisions about her life and whatever she chooses will be good for me. I also told her I am making my own choices.

I want my life to be simple and effortless the way it was in Paris. You and I were both true to ourselves. Everything became magical. All I would have to do when I touched you was to pay attention to the reaction of your body and your skin. It told me where to go and where not to go. I just had to stay present. I let myself be guided by my instincts and intuition.

By contrast, I see that I wasn't sufficiently honest and clear with Sabine before, but now I'm ready to go talk to her again.

Zacharie:
I just had a long talk with Sabine.

Anamika:
What did you discuss this time?

Zacharie:
I told her I wanted to take a trip by myself this summer.

Anamika:
How did she react?

Zacharie:
She was surprised and even shocked. It seemed very sudden to her. She seems to think I've become mentally unbalanced!

Anamika:
How funny! It's quite the opposite.

Zacharie:
I agree. I think I'm finally becoming sane!

Zacharie's conversations with Sabine went on and on like a good soap opera. As difficult as they were for him, they kept me entertained.

Zacharie:
I spoke to Sabine again. I said that I want to go to the United States this summer. She was angry and upset that we won't be spending our summer vacation together. Now she really thinks I have lost my mind. She asked where this crazy idea came from.

Anamika:
Did you tell her about me?

Zacharie:
No. I told her I need to follow my own desires and do what feels good to me.

Anamika:
It's great that you are starting to talk about coming to the United States. But unless you're willing to break the co-dependence with her, you're still not at liberty to come. That's what you keep avoiding.

Your dependence on her comes from not feeling whole, loved, and safe right now. This creates a black hole of neediness that can never be filled. Then you hold on to her to try to fill this hole.

Zacharie:
That's what I've been doing for 25 years.

Anamika:
The need for love is real, but it doesn't work to try to get love, safety, and satisfaction from someone or something external. Our needs can never be met that way and that hole can never be filled, no matter how hard we try.

Zacharie:
Is that why I still feel insecure and long to be free?

Anamika:
Yes. True freedom comes from growing beyond the belief that our needs must be met from the outside.

Zacharie:
Do you mean that everything I am longing for is already inside of me?

Anamika:
What everyone longs for is to feel loved, safe, and valued. We all actually have an infinite source of love and safety available inside of us. What if you could experience wholeness

inside of you right now? When you're resonating with that, you feel your needs met.

Zacharie:
How can I feel that?

Anamika:
When you stay in your head you believe you're not enough. You're not feeling your own infinite delicious flow of inner resource. To experience who you truly are, you need to sense and feel the substance, light and movement within.

Zacharie:
Oh, you mean like when we connect and I feel energy and emotions moving in my body?

Anamika:
Exactly! For example, what are you feeling right now?

Zacharie:
I can feel a knot inside my stomach, like I haven't really cut the cord with Sabine...

Anamika:
Recognizing what's binding you is the first step.

Zacharie:
I've been holding on to her as "mom" to try to give me confidence. But obviously, that hasn't worked. I want to experience that confidence in myself. When I'm with you, I connect with the energy within me, and it lifts my heart. That's when I feel confident. But I don't want to be with you because I need that from you. I want to be with you by choice and not by necessity.

Anamika:
That's real freedom!

Zacharie:
I understand there is no real love without real freedom. Maybe there is no freedom without love, either. I don't know.

Zacharie:
I just had conversation number 15 with Sabine. We went to dinner with a friend who is a psychoanalyst. I told him I was going to the United States this summer. He asked me why. I explained that I wanted to expand my horizons. He understood and said it sounded like

a great idea. His response was very accepting. After dinner, Sabine said his response helped her better understand my needs.

Z: Sabine confessed that she was scared about losing everything if I met someone this summer.

A: She's never asked you if you've met someone already?

Z: No. Like me, she doesn't want to know.

A: Oh my God! Do you think maybe the two of you really haven't wanted to know yourselves and each other?

Z: You're right, number 843. I understand that now because you and I do know each other, and now I'm just eager to be with you.

A: Me too! I crave you deadly!

Zacharie:
I just spoke to Sabine. I decided to continue to live with her for now and see what happens after my trip. We reviewed who we had been together and what was good. I told her that I don't know who I'll be after the trip and we'll need to evaluate our relationship then.

This gave me the sense of internal freedom I need to come to Malibu.

Anamika:
How did she receive what you said?

Zacharie:
Not so bad this time. She said she wants to be open to something new in her life as well.

Anamika:
Wonderful! You're liberating both of you! How do you feel after this talk?

Zacharie:
Relieved.

Anamika:
I'm so happy for you! It seems a big burden has been lifted.

Zacharie:
Yes. You being true to yourself has been helping me a lot and I hope the good things happening in my life help you as well. I can't wait to see you in Malibu!

Throughout his Sabine conversations, I know I kept asking him if he had truly cut the ties. I knew he was still attached to Sabine, but it was okay with me. He had clarified their relationship sufficiently for us to be together in Malibu.

I know this might seem unconventional, but for me, our connection was about exploration and discovery. In light of this, it didn't really matter that what we had together wasn't defined. What did matter was continuously becoming free.

CHAPTER 13

coming to malibu

A: I went to Sue's birthday party last night. I was imagining you being there with me. Every year on the evening of her birthday she has a gathering with dear friends. Maybe you can come with me next year?

Z: What will be the date of her birthday next year?

A: The same date as this year, of course.

Z: That's very strange, because last year on the same date it was also her birthday!

Once Zacharie decided he was coming, I was very excited. However, true to form, all of a sudden I didn't find him attractive anymore. He wasn't enough this or that, and I projected all of my own self-judgment onto him. It was just like before I went to Paris–all over again!

I was walking on the beach at Paradise Cove and comparing him to every muscular male beach body I saw. There are plenty of them in Paradise Cove, hence the name. One of these beach bodies actually struck up a conversation with me, and I quickly realized there was nobody home.

That woke me up. I remembered the richness of what Zacharie and I have together and couldn't wait for him to arrive.

Zacharie:
This trip is exciting but also frightening. But, at this point, the excitement is stronger than the fear. I seem to be turning a corner. I'm also afraid that when the trip is over, I won't want to leave Malibu.

Anamika:
I might not want you to leave either.

Z: I just dropped off my passport application.

A: Did you ask for a rush job?

Z: Yes, I asked, but they told me I would need a good reason.

A: You have two good reasons. You're coming to visit me and to learn more English!

Z: Romance is not a good enough reason for these officials.

A: Your romantic nature convinced me, so maybe it will convince them, too!☺

Anamika:

You look a little stressed. When you get to Malibu, maybe we can do a detox. That will make you feel better. What's that concerned look on your face? You have reservations?

Zacharie:
Yes, my plane leaves from Paris on June 30th at 8am.

Anamika:
How funny! In this context reservations means your concerns about the detox I suggested.

Zacharie:
Oh! Well, I have those reservations too!

A: I like speaking to you when I wake up and go to bed. It's a nice rhythm.

Z: It's so hard not to be with you in the morning, and in the evening… and in the day. Apparently, I want to spend all of my time with you.☺

A: Good morning, my sweetie.

Z: Shower time. Good time for thinking of you in a special way.☺

A: How? Wet and soapy? Are you naked?

Z: No, this morning I am going to take my shower dressed, and with an umbrella.

A: Here's your morning wake up hug, cutie pie.

Z: I had a very simple but exciting dream last night.

A: What did you dream?

Z: We were making love by the ocean in Malibu. It seemed so real, it waken me up.

A: It woke you up, remember?

Z: Crazy verb!

Z: I always become excited instantly when I hear your voice. *Oh, je t'aime ma chérie*. I love you, my sweetheart. Everything is so interesting when I'm with you.

Z: I want to take a shower with you with my umbrella.

A: You are so crazy.☺

Z: I know, but you love me crazy. So maybe you are the one who's crazier!

A: Perhaps, but you are quite nutty.

Z: What is the meaning of nutty in English?

A: It's endearing, like you have a screw loose in your head.

> **Z:** In French we say, "*avoir une araignée au plafond,*" to have a spider on the ceiling.
>
> **A:** Then you must have a million spiders on the ceiling of your head!

Zacharie:
The closer it gets, the harder it is to wait. I wish I were there already. I long for your body so much.

Anamika:
What is it you long for?

Zacharie:
The pleasure we both get when I touch you.

Anamika:
How beautiful! Usually someone would say I long to touch your hair or your legs.

Zacharie:
You mean I long to touch the hair on your legs?

Anamika:
Hair <u>or</u> legs!

Zacharie:
No, it's both. Every time I touch you, I'm surprised all over again. I seem to know exactly how and where to touch you.

Anamika:
When we connect in the flow of energy and follow its currents, it guides us. I long for your physical hands touching me as well. Waiting is a sweet torture, a delicious agony.

> **Z:** Today, I am going to the bank to ask for some dollar.
>
> **A:** <u>Dollars</u>.
>
> **Z:** No "s" needed because I will order only one.
>
> **A:** Only one? You are so crazy, the spiders on your ceiling must have multiplied.
>
> **Z:** I used to be very seri-

```
ous. No spiders on my ceil-
ing until I met you.

A: I wonder what that says
about me!
```

Zacharie:
I'm in resistance!! I had a bad dream last night about a snowstorm in the middle of summer that prevented me from going to Malibu. When I woke up I couldn't find my cell phone charger, so I couldn't send you a text. Then, I bought a new suitcase but forgot to ask for the keys. I can't open it.

Anamika:
Maybe there are no keys. Try the combination lock.

Zacharie:
Oh yes, that works! How funny, just today I reproached my students for not being more attentive. *Où ai-je encore mis ma tête?* Where did I put my head?

Anamika:
Look on top of your shoulders!

Zacharie:
Maybe I've lost my head because one year ago I was a different man. And I can imagine that a few months from now I'll be a completely new man again.

Anamika:
Sabine won't recognize you when you return.

Zacharie:
Sabine won't be home when I return. She decided to take a trip herself. I was a bit afraid about coming back without her there, but now I'm relieved.

Z: I feel so confident today.

A: What happened?

Z: It's as if I was asleep before in my life, and I just woke up.

A: Oh, your favorite crazy verb! You got it right!!!

Z: I said it right?

A: Yes, bravo!! You and I have both waked up more. Or is it awaken? Or is it awokened? Crazy verb!

CHAPTER 14

torture or figs

Z: The changes are very fast now. I am the same, but I'm not the same at all. I'm so glad to be who I've become, and I look back with tenderness at the person who first spoke to you on Skype.

A: The man with the basket on his head?

Z: Yes, I took the basket off and woke up to a whole world of possibility and freedom.

Zacharie was scheduled to arrive in two weeks. I was feeling extremely free of the concerns I had before Paris. I wasn't trying to make him "The One," nor was I pushing him away. I felt ready to be real and present together.

He felt the same way, open to experiencing. What fun to be available to limitless possibility!

Anamika:
Now that we're going to be together again, I'm reflecting upon the meaning of our connection.

Zacharie:
For me, there was something missing in my life, but I wasn't aware of it. A man from the Middle Ages can't dream of a TV set because it doesn't exist yet. You helped me be aware of things I didn't know existed.

With you, I'm on a journey. It doesn't seem to matter how it unfolds because it feels so good.

When I'm not following my heart, I can feel it inside me and I have the courage to make a different choice.

Anamika:
You have been such a catalyst for me, too. I have never felt this much love and freedom simultaneously. When I think of you coming

to Malibu, the ground begins to tremble with possibility.

Zacharie:
Are you having an earthquake?

Anamika:
Only inside. There's such exquisite pleasure with you. Can you feel the earthquake?

Zacharie:
We don't have them near Paris, but I can feel it anyway. *L'énergie circule divinement entre nous.* The energy circulates divinely between us. *Je t'aime comme un fou!* I love you like crazy! Let's stay together like this all night with these waves of energy and particles of light exploding in our bodies.

Anamika:
Now you are speaking like a Physicist and Metaphysician. I love it! We are opening through portal after portal into higher and higher states of ecstatic boundlessness together.

Zacharie:
Nous serons bientôt ensemble. We will be together very soon.

Anamika:
Speak to me in French, my favorite language of love.

Zacharie:
Quand je plonge les yeux dans ton regard, je suis envahi par une douceur infinie. Alors je t'embrasse si fort que nos deux corps ne sont plus qu'un et nous sommes entraînés dans une danse passionnée.

When he speaks to me like that in French, it sweeps me off my feet. I couldn't wait to hear him speak French in person.

Finally, Zacharie arrived. I picked him up at the Los Angeles International Airport, and we stood in the terminal holding each other for a long time just to make sure it was real.

We drove up the Pacific Coast Highway in my convertible to Malibu. Looking out at the ocean, he noticed, "Everything is so spacious and full of light."

It was fantastic to have him there, but I couldn't help noticing –those eyebrow hairs! The first thing I did when we got home was to go after them with a pair of scissors. That wasn't enough. I put bleach on his teeth and forced him to hike in the mountains or walk on the beach every single day. I fed him seaweed, but the good kind!

"This is torture!" he complained. "I'm taking the next plane home." It reminded me of my first night in Paris. "And if there's no flight," he persisted, "I'll walk or swim..."

After an arduous hike, we would sit on my deck overlooking the ocean and treat ourselves to figs, his favorite food. Shaqqara and Thor would always join us. Zacharie was discovering that he loved moving his body. *Je me sens si bien.* I feel so good. *Maintenant, je préfère tes tortures aux figues.* Now, I love your torture more than figs.

He looked out over the canyon and breathed deeply. "Being here is changing me," he said. "It's making me aware that I've invested so much in my relationship with Sabine and I feel like I've failed. I'm scared to start all over again."

"I've known that kind of failure many times," I told him, "because something has to die for something else to be born. Failure in this case just means that you've outgrown the way you've been."

He thought for a moment. "I can't imagine anything new growing out of what Sabine and I have."

"Perhaps you could continue to live with her as a friend? Maybe you will find a new emotional connection with her and go deeper? Or, you might both decide to live alone or with someone else, and continue your friendship. There are so many potential options for the future," I suggested. "Why don't you hold this situation in your heart with the possibility of an optimal outcome?"

He thought about that for a moment. "What if I left my life in France to come here and be with you, and then you abandoned me after three months?"

"I'm not the source of your love or security," I gently reminded him. Can you go beyond trying to control your life?"

"How do I do that?" he wanted to know.

"Could you loosen your grip, come down out of your head, and connect with the softness of your heart?" I suggested.

"That's easier said than done," he replied.

"That's your resistance and it's okay to include that part of you that wants to stay in control," I reminded him. "If you are willing to accept its presence with compassion, you will feel your inner flow, which is big enough to hold the control too."

"What you mean is, if I accept all of me, then I will create a beautiful future beyond what I can imagine?" he asked.

"Yes, exactly! How does that feel?"

"So much better!"

Shaqqara got up from her hammock and put her head in his lap. She let him stroke her head, something she doesn't do with anyone. He smiled at her and took my hand.

A few days later, it became unseasonably cool in Malibu. Zacharie, Shaqqara, Thor and I were cuddling under a down quilt. Zacharie seemed pensive. "What are you thinking about?" I asked.

"I feel so much stronger now," he replied. "France and Sabine seem far away. Life is easy and colorful here. I want to live in a way that is better for my physical and emotional wellbeing. I grow here every day internally and externally. I don't know who I'll be by the end of the trip, but in this moment I'm not worried about the future."

The next day we were sitting on the couch drinking hot lemon water and Zacharie was massaging my feet with his warm hands. I felt sad thinking about how much I would miss him when he returned to France. When I realized I was worrying about the future, I brought my attention back to the moment. Rays of sunlight were streaming through the window caressing my face. I suddenly felt a limitless space open up inside of me that was filled with substance, warmth, and light. It felt like the essence of freedom itself.

I surrendered into it. I let go of any need to know the outcome with Zacharie and how our lives might unfold. There are infinite possibilities within the unknown beyond the mind, beyond control, and beyond limited perspectives.

I realized that one of the most valuable gifts of our relationship was connecting with infinite possibility. I was basking in its joy, magic and mystery.

"I'm imagining being an astronaut," I mused aloud, "who is experiencing weightlessness for the first time. At first, I feel a fear of the unknown and want to feel safe in gravity again. Eventually my body and psyche acclimate and I learn to navigate in weightlessness. I'm discovering the safety in lightness."

"I wonder what it would be like walking in space?" Zacharie joined my reverie. "It sounds like fun as long as you're securely tethered to the spaceship."

"What if I could let go of my tether and spacesuit and experience floating freely in the luscious lightness of the unknown?" I imagined.

"It would be scary and thrilling at the same time," he responded, "but I'd like to experience it with you."

"In this eternal and infinite space," I reflected, "our experience would have no end."

CHAPTER 15

so much more

One night, sitting on Malibu's cliffs watching dolphins play during a particularly spectacular sunset, we were reviewing our year together.

"What was your impression the first time we met on Skype?" I asked Zacharie.

"I was agreeably surprised by what you looked like," he replied, "because as I told you, your photo didn't correspond with what your audio recording made me feel. I was happy that the warm impression I had from your voice was confirmed by your physical appearance and presence. You were so charming and I liked the way you moved and reacted to what I said."

"When you first saw me in person on the Internet, did you think I was physically attractive?" I persisted.

He thought for a moment and then said, "I wasn't really paying attention to your appearance. It wasn't external beauty I was looking for. For me, beauty corresponds with a person's energy, not only with their physical appearance."

"Do you remember the first time you told me you were living with someone?" I asked.

"Yes. You accepted that with ease and it was clear you weren't looking for a romantic relationship," he replied.

"Remember, the Moroccan guy? I was so glad you weren't like him," I laughed.

"Many people on the site weren't looking to study language," he said. "They were looking for a relationship. When they found out I was in a relationship, that was the end of the language study."

He turned to me, "What was your first impression of me?"

"I liked your sense of humor," I replied without having to think.

"The fact that you found me funny was very important to me," he explained, "because not everybody necessarily appreciates my humor. Despite the language difference, I felt like we really understood each other. I appreciated our first conversation and wanted to continue. But I wasn't sure if you would have the time and interest."

"I felt mysteriously comfortable with you," I responded. "You were kind-hearted, intelligent even though shy. You seemed very present in our conversation, and very willing. I liked that."

"It seemed that you and I were looking for the same thing," he commented.

"You were only looking for someone with whom to learn English?" I teased.

"Yes," he replied, "but I also wanted someone interesting to learn English with, whose conversation could bring something of quality and value into my life. Otherwise, it wasn't worth the time. In hindsight, I see that I was really looking for something much deeper, and English was the vehicle. I was really looking to learn about myself, even though I wasn't conscious of it at the time."

"Paradoxically," he laughed, "if I had consciously sought that out, I would never have gone to an Internet language site. I could never have imagined the man I've become."

"English Lessons," I joked, "and some lessons in language too." We looked at each other and laughed.

"We were both looking for something and we didn't know what it was," I added. "I knew you could help me with French, which you did magnificently, but I had no idea I would also find so much more."

"French Lessons," he said in his charming accent, "and some lessons in language too."

"Zacharie, we are both space explorers letting go of our tethers into the lightness of the unknown. It is beyond form and definition, beyond English and French, and beyond any known story. We are part of all that is..."

"Yes," he replied, "and so much more..."

I dropped Zacharie off at the Los Angeles International Airport early in the morning. It was still dark. We held each other for a long time not wanting to say goodbye. When I got home it was not yet light and the house was empty and cold. I cried my heart out.

As the sun began to rise I climbed the steep hill next to my house with Thor by my side. I looked out over the beautiful ocean illuminated by the sun's early rays and stared out into space. It was time to let go of my spacesuit and tether. With trepidation, I took a deep breath, opened my hands skyward and let go. I stepped out into the vast unknown. I was learning to navigate in luminous weightlessness, freedom and joy… and so much more…

17751776R00121

Made in the USA
San Bernardino, CA
16 December 2014